Jesuit Lives
at home in the world

Edited by Patrick Carberry SJ

Published by Messenger Publications, 2019
Copyright © Irish Province of the Society of Jesus, 2019

ISBN 978 1 788120 32 6

Designed by Messenger Publications Design Department
Maps reproduced by permission of Barry L Ruderman Antique Maps Inc.
www.RareMaps.com
Typeset in Adobe Caslon Pro
Printed by Hussar Books

Messenger Publications,
37 Lower Leeson Street, Dublin D02 W938
www.messenger.ie

It is according to our vocation to travel to any part of the world where there is hope of God's greater service and the help of souls.
Gerónimo Nadal SJ (1507–1580)

CONTENTS

FOREWORD

In 1539, a group of ten men gathered in Rome, among them Ignatius Loyola, to decide their future. It was a critical moment for them. The Pope was about to deploy them in small groups to different cities, and they had to decide if they should simply go their separate ways or try to remain together in one body. In spite of their diverse origins and their imminent dispersion, they decided that they should strive to maintain their union. Their reason is clearly expressed in a record they kept, *The Deliberation of the First Fathers*: 'In as much as our most kind and affectionate Lord had deigned to gather us together and unite us, men so spiritually weak and from such diverse geographical and cultural backgrounds, we ought not split apart what God has gathered and united.' Rather, they continued, 'we ought day by day to strengthen and stabilise our union, rendering ourselves one body with special concern for each other.' Their decision resulted, a year later, and after further determinations, in the founding of the Society of Jesus.

Unity and diversity: from the beginning that tension has been a characteristic of the Jesuits. As they spread across Europe and well beyond – to Asia, the Americas, Africa and Australasia – the cultural and linguistic diversity the Jesuits encountered was far greater than anything the first companions could have imagined. The bewildering variety of situations they faced gave rise to sometimes unexpected demands, and these frequently elicited creative responses. From the beginning, the Jesuits were defined, not by any particular ministry, but by an apostolic flexibility, a readiness to adapt to the concrete circumstances of time and place. Embodying a kind of restlessness, their desire was to go wherever the need was great and opportunities promising. What they were to do remained to be discovered, in the light of each situation.

It's not surprising, then, to find Jesuits engaged in a wide range of ministries and with many different stories to tell. A small sample of these stories can be read in these pages. Among their ranks, there have been visionary missionaries, like Matteo Ricci, while others, like Bernard Lonergan, have confined themselves largely to research, writing and the lecture hall. Some Jesuits, like Alberto Hurtado, have been leaders in implementing the social gospel in innovative ways, while others – John Sullivan comes to mind – have worked quietly and unobtrusively to bring hope into the lives of individuals and families in need. Many of the Jesuits featured in this volume were engaged at some stage in the formation of youth, which is not surprising, since education at all levels has been a major concern of the Jesuits from very early days. And, of course, there have been those Jesuits, like Ignacio Ellacuría, who have paid the ultimate price for their determination to announce the Good News in the face of violent opposition from vested interests.

What unites this body, with all its diversity, is what St Ignatius calls 'our way of proceeding'. This involves, first of all, a personal commitment to Jesus and the Gospel, as mediated through the eyes of Ignatius. With the *Spiritual Exercises* and the *Constitutions* to guide them, Jesuits are encouraged to walk with Jesus through all the phases of his life, making his vision and values their own, not just intellectually but affectively as well. In companionship with him, they are challenged to grapple with the disordered affections in their lives – and these are often stubbornly deep-seated – so as to embrace the kind of freedom that will enable them wholeheartedly to pursue God's will. Personal discernment, openness with superiors and, ultimately, obedience point a way forward that Jesuits are invited to embrace with confidence. Finally, as they carry out their mission, Jesuits bring with them the consolation, learned from the Exercises, of knowing that everything is gift, that God is present and active at all times and in all places, and that ultimately they are never in an alien world.

Patrick Carberry SJ
Editor

PART ONE
Africa

~ 1 ~
Beyond the Zambezi:
Joseph Moreau SJ (1864–1949)

Brendan Carmody SJ

Joseph Moreau was born at La Bruffière, Montaigu, in the region of Nantes in western France on 12 January 1864. Being of peasant stock, he was well acquainted with the demands of life on the farm, something he would put to good use later in life. He received his early education at Chavagnes-en-Paillers, some fifteen kilometres from his home, in a school conducted by a religious society known as the Chavagnes Priests. He later studied at a minor seminary in Sables d'Olonne, a seaside town about eighty kilometres from his home.

At the age of eighteen, Joseph made a retreat under the direction of a Jesuit, and it appears that it was in the course of this retreat that he first discussed his idea of becoming a priest. The retreat director wisely advised him to take some time before making a decision, and he encouraged him to attend the Jesuit apostolic school at Poitiers where he could further ponder the possibility of such a vocation.

During his time in Poitiers, Joseph read a recently published book called *Trois Ans dans l'Afrique Australe*, describing the beginnings of the Jesuits' Zambezi mission a few years earlier. This book made a deep impression on Joseph, and at the end of the year 1883, he applied to be admitted as a novice to the Society of Jesus. Shortly afterwards he started his two-year novitiate in Drongen, Belgium. Already as a novice, no doubt with *Trois Ans dans l'Afrique Australe* in mind, he expressed an interest in being assigned to the Zambezi Mission.

This mission, which the Church had entrusted to the Jesuits, covered a large territory in Central Africa. Initially manned by an international group of Jesuits, in the 1880s the administration of the mission was given over to the Jesuits' English Province (as it was then called). The vast region stretched from what today is the Democratic Republic of Congo, to south of the Limpopo river in the northern part of South Africa.

Mission to Africa

Shortly after the completion of his novitiate, and while still in his studies, Joseph's wish was granted. A small group of Jesuits, consisting of one priest and five scholastics, was sent to South Africa and among them was Joseph Moreau. One can imagine the psychological challenge this journey must have presented for the six inexperienced Frenchmen. In the years before air travel, trips of this nature would take three or four weeks, during which contact with the outside world would become increasingly difficult. Entering a territory largely unknown to them, the places they travelled through must have appeared strange. While European knowledge of the African interior had improved following the missionary explorations of the Scottish Presbyterian, David Livingstone (1813–1873), in reality relatively little was known in the Europe of that time about this vast continent and its peoples.

In South Africa, Joseph studied philosophy at Dunbrody, on the Eastern Cape. This was followed, as part of his formation as a Jesuit, by three years' teaching. During that period, in his spare time, Joseph studied Xhosa, a widely spoken language in that region. This was an important step, since Xhosa would give him a structure and framework for learning other languages in the Bantu group. With this foundation, he later mastered three other major languages, SiNdebele and ChiShona, spoken in what is now Zimbabwe, and Chitonga, spoken in the southern part of present-day Zambia.

After his years of teaching, Joseph was sent to study theology at St Buenos in Wales. He was ordained priest in 1896, and in the following year he made his Tertianship, the final phase of a Jesuit's formation. Having completed this period of spiritual and apostolic renewal, Moreau returned to South Africa, leaving family, friends and homeland once again. From his letters, we know that he always maintained a keen interest in what was happening to his own country and people, especially during the two World Wars. Much later, when he was in his early sixties, he contemplated a visit back to France to see his family, but on reflection he felt that the journey would be too much for him. He also feared that the prospect of bidding his people farewell for the last time was something he could not face. So, like many missionaries of that era, he was never to set foot again in his home country.

A Treacherous Journey

After his return to Africa as a young priest, Joseph spent some time at Bulawayo, Gweru and Chishawasha, all in the region of Harare. He found himself restless, however, haunted by a desire to explore that part of Africa further north, and to extend the Jesuit mission beyond its then frontiers. Presumably he let these desires be known to his superiors, for he was sent in 1902 with an English Jesuit, Fr Peter Prestage, to prospect for a mission north of the river Zambezi. They were not the first Jesuits to undertake this dangerous task. There had been earlier Jesuit expeditions in this area that had been unsuccessful, mainly due to the devastating effects of malaria and blackwater fever, diseases which were almost impossible to remedy and which cost many lives.

Setting out towards the Victoria Falls – a trek of some 700 kilometres – Moreau and his companion sometimes travelled by ox wagon but most of it was done on foot. It was a treacherous journey through bush paths, negotiated with only the most basic instruments to keep them on track. At night, they slept in makeshift tents or under the clear, starry African sky. As the sun set, all noise died down, except for the mysterious sounds of life stirring in the dark shadows, the occasional crack of a branch, the rustle of feet or the swirl of water in a nearby stream. There was also the unwelcome interruption of buzzing mosquitoes and bellowing bush-buck, and occasionally the stomping of a curious elephant or the roar of a hungry lion. No doubt, all these creatures wondered what these invaders were up to, and danger was never too far away. If there was any compensation for the hardships Moreau and his companion endured, it was surely to be found in the beauty of the sky. There is no moon like an African moon: huge, glowing and alive; and there is no sky as magnificent as an African sky: velvet deep and eloquently silent.

From Victoria Falls to Monze

Eventually, Moreau and Prestage arrived at the Victoria Falls, no doubt overawed by the incredible cascade of water and the deafening roar it made as it plunged into the vast ravine below. They found that a bridge over the falls was under construction, connecting what was then Southern and Northern Rhodesia, but it had not yet been completed. To cross the enormous stretch of the Zambezi, Moreau and Prestage had to search for a sufficiently shallow spot in order to wade across in relative safety, hoping that they hadn't been eyed by a hippopotamus or crocodile on the way.

After crossing the Zambezi, they set out north for Kalomo, about 140 kilometres away, where the British South Africa Company (BSAC), a private enterprise developed by Cecil Rhodes and the government of the territory, had its administrators. There they met the governor, Sir Robert Coryndon, and the chief administrator, Stephen Lanigan O'Keefe, both of whom welcomed the mission party and encouraged them to press on. Lanigan O'Keefe proposed a site for a mission station some fifty kilometres east of Kalomo, but Moreau and Prestage had their doubts about the location. They felt that it would be preferable to stay closer to the railway line that was being constructed at the time, and so the mission group decided to go further north, to Monze, which meant a further trek of about 150 kilometres.

On arrival in Monze, the two Jesuits were well received by the chief and elders. Chief Monze, who had met the great explorer David Livingstone when he had passed by in the 1840s, appeared to be an open kind of man, with his European shoes and clothes. With the help of an interpreter, whom they had brought with them from the Victoria Falls, the Jesuits explained their motive for coming and their hopes for the future. The chief was impressed by them and by what they were planning to do, and he agreed to allow four local boys, one of them his own son, to accompany them back to Southern Rhodesia to help them with their preparations for a permanent settlement in Monze. The boys, aged between eleven and seventeen, were Bbinya (the chief's son), Haatontola, Jojo and Jahaliso. Before they left, Moreau pegged out a site near Monze which he hoped would be the location of the future mission.

With great excitement, the party set out for Empandeni in Southern Rhodesia, where a Jesuit mission had already been established. In Empandeni, their plan was study Chitonga and become proficient in it, and to make plans for the future mission. And that is what they did. For the next three years, the boys taught Moreau their language while he taught them English, the basics of the faith, and some practical skills. They were baptised at Christmas 1904.

Preparing for the Mission

On 21 June 1905, three years after his first visit to Monze, Moreau and another French Jesuit, Jules Torrend, together with the Tonga boys, took the train to the Victoria Falls. This time, they were allowed to cross the bridge, although it was still unfinished and quite dangerous. As Moreau recalled: 'The construction of the bridge started from both sides of the river at the same time, and the two parts of the bridge, like two giant men stretching across their long ponderous arms towards one another, had joined hands across the abyss. One could, if one liked and was allowed, walk over the awe-inspiring chasm.' At their own risk, the party walked across the the unfinished structure, above the gorge into which the mile-wide Zambezi hurled its furious waters more than a hundred metres below. It seems that they made the crossing without incident.

From the Falls, they took the train towards Kalomo, along the newly built line, and then they hired a wagon and oxen that would take them to Monze, a ten-day journey. On reaching Monze, they were shocked to find that all was not well. The old chief, who had welcomed them so warmly on their earlier visit, was now in prison for some petty crime. This greatly saddened everyone, his son Bbyinya in particular. They also discovered that some days before their arrival, the site they had chosen for the mission had been handed over to another missionary group, the Seventh Day Adventists. They had to start all over again.

Moreau was undaunted, however. Being a man of deep faith, he reasoned that God did not always write in straight lines, and so he and Torrend set out confidently to find another site. After some days, they found a good spot some 12 kilometres away at the confluence of the Magoye and Chikuni rivers, in an area ruled by Chief Siantumbu. There, Moreau and his party pitched camp. 'On the night of July 14, 1905,' Moreau was later to write, 'the Chikuni mission was born, not even in a stable but in the open air under a tall, unsheltering musekese tree'. It was the middle of the cold season, and the the night was chilly, but it marked the eve of a new day for the Catholic Church and for Tongaland.

Establishing the Mission

Moreau and his companions had arrived, but now they faced the challenge of setting up a mission station in the middle of the bush. Their first task was to build simple huts of clay and wattle in which to live. Not long afterwards, however, with the aid of builders from Bulawayo, they began to plan more substantial houses. The builders' construction method, involving baked mud bricks and zinc roofs, amazed the local people, for whom this method was new. Among the many constructions started at this time, the church, completed in 1911, had pride of place. Regretably, only part of the bell tower still stands today, but it remains a notable landmark in the area.

This little oasis became the nucleus of Fr Moreau's mission to the Tonga people, and very soon they were celebrating Mass regularly, especially on Sundays and Church feasts.

From such small beginnings, the mission station began to grow into what is today the diocese of Monze, with a Catholic population of about 400,000, consisting of twenty-two parishes, fifty-five priests and 121 sisters. The mission station itself now includes a parish church, a hospital, a secondary school for boys and another for girls, as well as a College of Education called after St Charles Lwanga.

A Revolution in Farming

Before any of that could happen, however, Moreau realised that he would have to ensure that the people had enough food and water to survive. The area had known many famines over the years, and people had very little food and only poor clothing. Early on, Moreau showed the way himself by growing vegetables and fruit, and especially maize, the staple diet of the people in that area.

Until then, the Monze people had only basic hoes with which to cultivate the soil. This meant that food production was slow and tedious, and could only cater for the family's own needs, at best. As someone who had been reared on a farm, Moreau realised that a plough could change all that very quickly. Within months, he had brought one from Bulawayo, and in the following rainy season a huge audience of local people gathered to watch in amazement as Moreau himself started ploughing with oxen. Soon, local leaders started to send oxen to Moreau to be trained and then returned to their owners.

As the years went by and their skills in ploughing increased, many local farmers became quite prosperous, selling some of their surplus produce for cash. Selling for money had become necessary only recently, when the BSAC government started imposing a tax on households. This was designed to force the younger generation to abandon their farms in order to work in the various mines that were being developed in the region – copper to the north and diamonds and gold to the south. The new prosperity of the farmers, however, meant that many of them could now pay the tax, stay at home and avoid the misery of the mines.

A Patient Approach

At first sight, it may seem strange that Moreau initially preoccupied himself with ploughing instead of preparing people for baptism. Indeed, even Moreau's superior rebuked him on one occasion for being primarily a farmer. Naturally, this irked Moreau, who defended himself by quoting the French proverb, *'Ventre affamé n'a point d'oreilles'* – a hungry stomach has no ears.

Moreau viewed himself as first and foremost a missionary, with a commitment to building up a local Church community, but he was a practical man. He knew intuitively that he had to start where the people were, not where he might like them to be. He had to address the needs of the whole person, beginning with the most fundamental need of all, nutrition. Hence the importance of the plough.

Moreau also knew that he had to exercise patience in preaching the Gospel. He realised that, in bringing the Good News to Monze, the Tonga people might not at first see the need for this strange and confusing religion. After all, they had their own religious system, with which they felt comfortable. To establish the mission on a firm basis, Fr Moreau realised that, besides prayer, he needed the support and cooperation of the local people. To achieve this, he regularly visited the local chiefs, and it seems that he became good friends with several of them. Moreau also frequently visited the local people in their homes, making sure to greet them in their traditional ritualistic way. In this respect, his French sense of politeness and respect no doubt helped.

Over time, Moreau's patient approach began to bear fruit. Most older people never did become Catholics. Those who were baptised were largely the young, who embraced the faith through a slow and complex process, inspired by the climate of trust and love which Moreau and his fellow missionaries radiated. The deepest impact on the younger generation often came through their experience of education in the schools.

The Importance of Education

Besides the personal contacts, which Moreau clearly recognised as essential, it was necessary also to build up a Church structure if the mission was to develop. As part of his plan, following the example of Bishop Shanahan in Nigeria, he founded a school, where people of all ages could learn to read and write. The school was to become a critical part of Moreau's vision but, as always, it demanded patience. It took time and persistence to entice local people to attend. The older people frequently saw no point in sitting in class learning European nonsense, when they could be doing better things. For a while, too, many younger people resisted the commitment and tedium that schooling required. They would come for a day or two, and then decide that they could employ themselves better in hunting or cattle herding.

In view of the importance they attached to education, Moreau and the other missionaries saw the employment of good teachers as essential, teachers who were competent to instruct their charges, not only in secular subjects, but in the rudiments of the faith as well. The missionaries themselves were few in number, and so they needed to look beyond themselves for assistance. For this purpose, they carefully selected local people as assistants, and these in time became pivotal to the success of the mission. Among these early catechists were the boys who had gone to Bulawayo with Moreau several years earlier, and who had become committed Catholics. They subsequently spent much of their lives building up the Church in Chikuni.

Moreau's concern for education was not limited to the male population of the area. In 1920 he invited the Sisters of Notre Dame de Namur to develop a school for girls, and they laboured in this field for nearly thirty years. At that point, Moreau's successor decided that higher levels of schooling were needed, and this was provided by the Irish Sisters of Charity, who developed a girls' secondary school, teacher training and a hospital, all of which have rendered great service to the local people. The presence of the sisters opened new horizons for Tonga girls who, instead of inevitably becoming housewives, now had an alternative: they could enter religious life. One of the first local congregations of sisters began at Chikuni in the 1940s, the Handmaids of the Blessed Virgin Mary.

Respect for the Local

A somewhat puzzling aspect of Moreau's behaviour is his refusal to teach the students English. His own grasp of the language was of the highest standard, having lived for many years in English-speaking environments. Nevertheless, he held out against its being taught in the mission. He feared, it seems, that by learning English the students would be tempted to go to the towns and mining centres for employment – he called this 'Bulawayo fever' – leaving their home territory deprived of their energy, and consequently remaining underdeveloped. Perhaps he was conscious, ahead of his time, of the dangers of what we today we term 'globalisation', with its tendency to stamp out the local way of life.

As a missionary in what was a British-ruled territory, Moreau was aware that he was in need of the goodwill of the colonial administrators. Cooperation with them was essential for the flourishing of the mission, even though his message – based on the fundamental freedom and dignity of every person – was at variance with theirs. Unlike them, he had not come to exploit the people, or to grab their resources. In this ambiguous situation, Moreau consciously maintained a distance from the colonial powers, refusing the proferred honour of an MBE on at least three occasions. At times, he protested against legislation that was adding to the people's burdens, especially the imposition of the 'hut tax' that was imposed on every household.

Consistent with his concern to preserve the people's way of life, Moreau not only took care to learn the Tonga language well but he also learned about and appreciated their customs. He chose a local word *Leza* to translate 'God' into Chitonga, judging that the people's traditional conception of God, as expressed by that word, was essentially the same as that of Christians. Pastorally, he was highly sensitive to the dilemma posed by some inherited traditions, such as polygamy, for those who became or wanted to become Catholic. When he joined his people at the rain shrine – the traditional place of prayer to the ancestors for rain – he told them, 'We all believe that our departed friends are still with us, and in this the Tonga think more highly than some who have come to preach the word of God … The dead who have died in a state of grace have gone to heaven; they can know us, hear us and intercede for us.'

Final Resting Place

It is surely not surprising that, when Moreau died on 20 January 1949, the people wanted to give him a traditional chief's funeral. They had considered him to be one of their own, and wanted to honour him now in a way he would certainly have greatly relished. In the event it did not happen. A downpour came as his funeral was about to take place, and the plans had to be changed at the last moment. Some of the missionaries present may have been pleased by this, perhaps even seeing it as a sign from heaven. That is surely not how Moreau would have seen it, nor is it the way many people today would view it. Openness, dialogue and respect across religious traditions are leading to a new kind of evangelisation, where Christianity can be experienced, not as something alien imposed from the outside, but as something that breathes the native air and takes root in the local soil. Moreau gave his life for this conviction.

As the shadows lengthened on that January day when Moreau was laid to rest in the local cemetery, there were many sad hearts among the Tonga people. They realised that they had lost a great friend who, as a Catholic missionary from far away, had brought them the Good News of Jesus Christ and helped them make it their own. He not only preached it; he lived its message of love in a way that generated new life. As the fever of his life ended and his work was done and as the mud on his grave settled, the Tonga people prayed that the Lord in his mercy would grant Fr Joseph Moreau a safe lodging, holy rest and peace.

PART TWO

Asia

~ 2 ~

Discovering the Chinese Christ:
Matteo Ricci SJ (1552–1610)

Thierry Meynard SJ

When I joined the Jesuits in France some thirty years ago, I was quite unfamiliar with the story of Matteo Ricci. Now, having lived in China for some twenty years, Ricci has become a real inspiration for me, as he is for many people there, four centuries after his death. I have come to appreciate how important Matteo Ricci still is for many Chinese people, far beyond the small Catholic community in China. Ricci represents a wonderfully positive encounter between China and the West, long before the traumatic experiences of colonisation in the nineteenth and twentieth centuries sullied the relationship. In presenting his life and work, I hope to explain how Ricci found the presence of God, the Chinese Christ, in the people of China.

Early Years

Matteo Ricci was born in 1552 in the small city of Macerata in central Italy, not far from the Adriatic Sea. At that time, the Jesuits had only come into being eight years earlier, and Ricci attended one of their earliest colleges, where he studied humanities. His father, an herbal pharmacist and member of the city council, hoping that

Matteo would assume an important role in the life of the city, sent him to La Sapienza University in Rome to study law.

Matteo had other ideas, however, and against his father's will he joined the Jesuits in 1571. After his novitiate, he received a broad training at the Jesuits' Roman College, which included philosophy, mathematics and astronomy. His request to be sent to the missions was granted, and he departed for the Far East from Lisbon in 1578. After spending some years in India, where he completed his theological studies and carried out some pastoral work, he arrived Macau, a Portuguese trading post, in 1582.

Learning to Respect the Culture

Some Westerners at that time, on coming to East Asia, dreamt about a military invasion on the model of the conquista in South America or in the Philippines, but most people realised that this model would not work in Japan or China. For their part, the Jesuits had learned their own lessons from the experience of St Francis Xavier and the companions who had accompanied him in Japan some decades earlier. They had arrived in 1549, and were successful in converting local feudal lords and quickly bringing about mass conversions but Christianity was not well integrated into the fabric of Japanese society, and had only shallow roots from which to grow.

Alessandro Valignano, the official Jesuit Visitor for all East Asia, realised that above all Christianity needed to be rooted in Asian culture if it was to flourish. Instead of missionaries proclaiming the Gospel through local catechists, as had been the practice, Valignano believed that Christianity needed first to be immersed within the local culture; it was on this rock, he believed, that evangelisation could be built. With this in mind, he organised a serious training program in philosophy and theology for young Japanese Jesuits that was adapted to their culture.

Valignano also wished to promote the project of St Francis Xavier who, in 1552, had died on Sancian Island off the coast of China, attempting to reach the Chinese mainland. For this purpose, he instructed Ricci and another recently arrived Jesuit, Michele

Ruggieri, to learn the Chinese language thoroughly. This may appear today as an obvious requirement, but back then many missionaries considered learning the language a waste of time, and were satisfied with very basic language skills in announcing the Gospel.

Putting down Deep Roots

Ruggieri accompanied the Portuguese merchants on their short business trips from Macau to Canton, but he was expected to return immediately with them, since foreigners were not allowed to settle in China. Despite that ban, however, the inspector general of the provinces of Guangdong and Guangxi made an exception: he allowed the Jesuits to take up residence in the city of Zhaoqing to practice their religious life, which he considered to be a variant of Buddhism. The exotic gifts the Jesuits brought with them from the West – such as clocks and musical instruments – played an important role in this development, as did their friendship with the prefect of Zhaoging. It signified a major breakthrough.

For any Westerner, learning Chinese is a schooling in humility and patience. When Ruggieri and Ricci started to learn the language, they could not rely on any manual or textbook, for there was none, so one of the first things they did was to write a dictionary for themselves. Furthermore, they quickly realised that it was not enough to learn the language as commonly spoken. In order to communicate effectively with the literati – the educated classes – they needed to reach a level of excellence in the language, because the future development of Christianity in China depended on the goodwill and official authorisation of this powerful group. Ruggieri and Ricci had to leave aside any dream they may have had of quick evangelisation. They would not be building churches with hundreds of worshippers in attendance.

Instead, they spent their time reading the Chinese classics and attempting to understand Confucian learning, especially the *Four Books* which were central to Chinese culture and which they started to translate into Latin. In the process, they discovered that the ancient Chinese texts already contained the concept of divinity;

more controversially, they also came to believe that the notion of God was properly expressed in Chinese as *Shangdi*, or the Lord-on-High.

A Controversial Issue

Valignano instructed Ricci to write a catechism that would incorporate passages from the Chinese classics, and this he undertook with enthusiasm. It took a lot of time and a lot of hard work. After ten years of study of the Chinese classics and dialogue with Confucian literati, whose help he used, Ricci published in 1603 *The True Meaning of the Lord of Heaven*, in which he proclaimed that the Christian God, the Lord of Heaven (*Tianzhu*), is the same as the *Shangdi* of the ancient Chinese texts.

This was a controversial issue. Ricci understood that linguistic and cultural mediations were necessary in order to talk about the Christian faith in a way the Chinese people could appreciate, and he accepted the risk of translating the concept of God into a different language and culture. Others, more cautious, rejected the risk altogether and insisted on using the Latin word *Deus*, which they transliterated into Chinese as *Dou-si*. Ricci's acceptance of *Shangdi* was based on his close study of Chinese texts and his deep understanding of them. It was not a resigned concession to the local culture. Nor was it a strategy for manipulating the Chinese language from within, twisting the original meaning into something completely different and colonising China, not through military weapons, but through ideological tools.

In fact, many people who analyse the interaction of Ricci with Chinese scholars are too rigid in their interpretation of that encounter, failing to consider the fact that both Ricci and the Chinese scholars were transformed through the dialogue. In this process, Ricci encountered the Chinese Christ, an experience by which he was himself altered and shaped by the Other. This was a truly Christian experience, which led Ricci to renounce, like Christ, the illusion of egotism and self-power, opening his life, through the mediation of others, to the presence of the Father in the Chinese culture.

Busy Years in Beijing

Through his writings, we can appreciate how open Ricci was to learning from this new culture and sharing it with others. In his memoirs, written at the end of his life, Ricci retraced his long and adventurous journey from south China up to Beijing, sharing all that he learnt about this new culture on the way. He expresses his amazement at the sophistication of its administration, for instance. He praises the civil examination system that allocates public functions in a fair way, while Europe was still using the hereditary system, or resorting to the purchase of public offices. He wonders at the social order he found in China at a time when Europe was being torn apart by wars. Ricci, as we can see, had largely left aside a Eurocentric vision of the world, and had enriched himself with all his discoveries.

In the spring of 1600, Ricci, carrying some gifts for the emperor, journeyed northwards from Nanjing. The journey was not without incidents and perils. He was held in jail in Tianjin for five months until, when the emperor heard that a foreigner had some gifts for him, he was finally allowed to proceed to Beijing. On 25 January 1601, Ricci presented his gifts, together with a written tribute, before the empty imperial throne. The emperor and the women of the palace were quite excited by those gifts, especially the two clocks whose hourly chimes intrigued them very much. Since the clocks contained complicated mechanisms, Ricci was allowed to prolong his stay in order to keep the clocks in good working order.

Ricci also carried with him a wealth of scientific knowledge, which the Chinese greatly appreciated. In many ways, the science he brought was more advanced than Chinese scientific studies, but Ricci never used his knowledge in an arrogant way to show his superiority, nor did he withhold information in order to appear better than the Chinese people. On the contrary, he freely communicated his knowledge to the many Chinese people who came to him. For example, he spent a few years teaching geometry to one of these students, Xu Guangqi, after which they produced together a translation of the Elements of Euclid.

While in Beijing, Ricci found himself particularly busy every third year, receiving in his residence hundreds of scholars who were arriving to take part in the national examination. They asked him questions about his map of the world, about how to compute the timings of eclipses of the sun or moon, and occasionally about theological issues. Ricci mentions in his letters that he often had no time for lunch and was forced to fast on these occasions, but he never tired of giving explanations to those who asked and joining in their conversations.

Ricci was fully aware that it would take much time for Christianity to become accustomed to China, and for China to become accustomed to Christianity. He was also careful not to shock the literati by discussing with them the crucifixion of Jesus and his Resurrection. Some other missionaries would criticise him for that, but Ricci was prepared to wait until they were ready to hear the message. For those who were ready, he would talk freely about those mysteries, and he would give them some catechetical texts that he had prepared for this purpose. Ricci's patient method of evangelisation reflects his respect for the Incarnation at work in the culture.

China's Impact on Ricci

Ricci had to reshape his identity as a Westerner, as a Jesuit missionary and as a priest. He had been sent by the Jesuit Order for the mission in China, and he kept in regular communication with Valignano and the superior general in Rome. From them he received instructions, guidelines and encouragements, and also the practical support of new Jesuits, finance and books. Ricci also wrote letters to his family members, teachers, fellow Jesuits and friends in Europe. Communication was slow and unreliable at that time, of course; a letter would usually take two years to arrive at its destination, and many were lost on the way. Only fifty-four letters of the many Ricci wrote have survived.

Ricci lived in isolation, some 2,000 kilometres away from Macau and often under the suspicion of being a foreign spy. He quickly understood that he needed the support of Chinese friends, and he developed a network of relationships that would protect him from being misunderstood or abused by some who were only interested in taking advantage of his expertise. It is quite significant that the first book Ricci wrote in China is his *Treatise on Friendship,* which earned him a lot of moral credit.

Another metamorphosis concerned his religious identity. When Ruggieri and Ricci arrived China, they naturally decided to adopt a clear religious identity. They wore the Buddhist garb, shaved their heads, and lived next to Buddhist temples. They shared with Buddhist monks many similarities, like the celibate life, community living, religious rituals and the reading of scriptures. By adopting the social trappings of Buddhism, the Jesuits made it clear from the start that they had come to China not for business or other secular aims but for religious reasons.

Nevertheless, their adoption of a pseudo-Buddhist identity created a lot of confusion, because Ruggieri and Ricci explicitly rejected core tenets of Buddhism, such as belief in reincarnation. Eventually, Ricci repudiated any association with Buddhism altogether. Indeed, from today's perspective, we can see that Ricci had a poor understanding of Buddhism. He inherited from his confrères in Japan their biased judgment about Buddhism as being either idolatrous or atheist. Having rejected any association with Buddhism, and probably following his Confucian interlocutors, Ricci developed a very harsh attitude towards Buddhist monks, as well as Taoist priests.

In 1595, Ricci left the Guangdong province, where he had spent twelve years, and he moved to the Jiangxi province. Along the way, he changed his social identity, dropping the Buddhist garb completely, and wearing instead the silk dress of the Confucian literati with its four-cornered hat. It was at this time that he grew the long beard that we know from his portrait. This bold decision, which was approved by Valignano, meant that Ricci entered further into a Confucian way of life, in which the delimitation between the secular and the sacred operate very differently than in the West. This meant that the sacred could be found in the secular, within the interplay of personal relationships regulated by the Confucian rituals.

It was in this context that Ricci came to understand the meaning of the rituals to the ancestors that were frequently practised in China. In front of the tablets of their parents and ancestors, Chinese people were not worshipping idols with supernatural powers, he believed, but they were expressing their connectedness with those who had transmitted life, culture and moral principles to them. Later, after Ricci's death, this issue – knows as the Chinese Rites Controversy – would become the focus of bitter controversy, as we shall see.

Despite the obvious limitations of the theology of his time, Ricci was able to engage in a fruitful experience, in which he encountered the Chinese Christ through his Chinese friends, through the teaching of Confucius, and through the moral and cultural ideals of China. Ricci was not only a great scholar of China and its language; he had a deep empathy for the people and for their culture, allowing them to effect in him a self-transformation. By discovering the Chinese Christ, Ricci enriched his own experience of Christ and was able to communicate it to others.

On one occasion, Ricci wrote that his time was not yet a time for reaping in China, nor even for sowing, but rather a time for clearing the woods. On another occasion, he wrote that the success of the Jesuits' apostolate should not be judged by counting the number of Christians only, but by the strength of the foundation they were establishing for a very big enterprise.

Appreciation for Ricci Today

After his death in 1610, Ricci's vision and practices were criticised and re-evaluated on many occasions. This was especially true during the Chinese Rites Controversy, when some missionaries in China were loud in opposition to Ricci's understanding of these practices. The controversy continued for many decades, until finally, in 1704, the pope condemned as superstitious the rituals offered to Confucius and the ancestors. These rituals, which were prescribed as normative by Chinese society, were now forbidden to Chinese Catholics. This provoked a reaction from the Chinese emperors, who ordered a stricter control over the Catholic Church, leading eventually its proscription. Many Chinese Catholics remained faithful, however, and practised their faith in a discreet way.

It was not until 1939 that the Chinese Rites were once again allowed to Catholics, by Pope Pius XII. Later, the Second Vatican Council returned to the underlying issue, when it stressed the importance of culture in evangelisation. From then on Ricci began to be seen as a model of what we know today as 'inculturation'. Twenty years after the council, the cause for Ricci's beatification was started in 1984, in the diocese of Macerata, and in 2013 it was transmitted to the Congregation for the Causes of Saints, where it is still in process.

In 2009, Pope Benedict XVI wrote of Ricci, 'What made his apostolate original, and we could say prophetic, was the profound sympathy he nourished for the Chinese, for their cultures and religious traditions ... Even today, his example remains as a model of a fruitful encounter between European and Chinese civilisations'. In 2016, Pope Francis echoed his predecessor's sentiments when he explained how he drew inspiration from Ricci, who showed the Church that 'it is necessary to enter into dialogue with China', because of its wealth of wisdom and history, as 'a land blessed with many things'. This is probably one of the deepest insights Ricci has to teach us: if God created the wonderful culture and traditions of China, then the Chinese cannot but have something to say about God himself. He was canonised by Pope Francis on 17 December 2013.

~ 3 ~

From Cork to China and Windsor Castle:
Thomas Ryan SJ (1889–1971)

Thomas J. Morrissey SJ

Windsor Castle, in the county of Berkshire in England, is the site of Queen Victoria's funeral, of many royal tombs and memorials and, of course, of royal weddings. It is surely surprising to find, in the midst of this royal splendour, a plaque to an unassuming Irishman from the rebel county:

> *Remember with Prayer and Praise*
> *THOMAS RYAN*
> *1889–1971*
> *who for thirty-eight years served his Lord in*
> *Hong Kong as Priest of the Society of Jesus.*

Many people must wonder who this Thomas Ryan was, and how he came to be commemorated in this prestigious place.

Early Years

Thomas Francis Ryan was born at Ballintemple, on the outskirts of Cork city, on 30 December 1889, the younger of two brothers. When he was only three years of age, his father died, leaving behind a young widow and two small boys. Fortunately, their mother had wealthy brothers who were generous to her, and the boys were able to attend Presentation Brothers College, where they completed their secondary education. Tom's brother went on to become a dentist, while Tom decided to join the Jesuits.

Following a noviceship of two years in St Stanislaus College in Rahan, near Tullamore, Tom spent two further years there studying literature and the humanities. He was then sent to Italy to study philosophy for three years at the Jesuit college in Udine. Being relatively close to Venice and Florence, Tom found himself in the midst of some of the world's great art works and, enthralled by them, he began to develop what became a lifelong interest. Returning to Ireland, he was assigned, as part of his Jesuit formation, to teach for four years at Belvedere College. It is a sign of his remarkable energy and ability that he managed during those years, in addition to his teaching duties, to study at University College Dublin, initially for a BA, and subsequently for an MA.

And that wasn't all. During his final two years in Belvedere, Tom edited the college annual, *The Belvederian*. It was a challenging time for an editor. Numerous past students were fighting in the Great War, and *The Belvederian* chronicled the deaths of many of them. The annual also paid attention to prominent past students on the nationalist side, such as Joseph Plunkett, Tom Humphreys, Cathal Brugha and Laurence O'Neill, the Lord Mayor of Dublin who was one of the leaders of the anti-conscription movement.

Following a further spell in Clongowes Wood College, Tom finally moved in 1921 to Milltown Park, Dublin, to commence his theological studies. Because of the troubled state of the country at the time, his ordination was brought forward, so that he was already a priest for most of his theological studies. On completion of his theology, in 1925, he was assigned to Paray-le-Monial in France for his Tertianship, the final year of his Jesuit training. At the end of that year, it was recorded that, in addition to his knowledge of Latin and Irish, he could speak French and Italian well, that he knew some German, and could read Spanish and Portuguese. His linguistic skills would stand to him in the future.

Social Commitment

After Tertianship, the young Fr Ryan was assigned to the Belvedere community once again, this time not to teach, but to be editor of two magazines, *The Irish Messenger of the Sacred Heart*, which had the widest circulation of any magazine in the country, and *Madonna*, concerned largely with devotion to Our Lady. In addition, he started and edited another publication, *The Irish Jesuit Directory and Year Book*, which continued to exist for many years.

As if that wasn't enough, he also found time to address a pressing concern of the time – the destitute of Dublin, and especially its poverty-stricken youth. Horrified by the extent of the deprivation he encountered, he berated the authorities by word and in writing for the terrible condition of Dublin's slums. His passion and energy were noted, and he was soon invited on to the Bench of the Juvenile Court, where he served for five years. During that time, he is said to have visited every remand home, reformatory and institute of detention in Ireland. He was strongly committed to the Belvedere Building Association, which provided flats for the poor. Among the poor he met were families of the boys in the Belvedere Newsboys' Club, to which he was appointed chaplain in 1927 and which became especially dear to him.

This club was concerned with the plight of the barefoot boys who sold newspapers in the city centre in order to generate some income for their families. The club provided them with warmth, food and a basic education. Fr Ryan visited each boy's home, got to know the parents and families, and acquainted himself with their struggles. If any boy was in difficulties with the law, he was prepared to go to court to speak on his behalf. None of this was forgotten. One club member, Jim Doyle, remained a life-long correspondent of Fr Ryan, and club members regularly sent good wishes to him.

Ryan's interest in social and economic issues led him to appreciate the papal social encyclicals, whose message he took to heart and promulgated enthusiastically. He called for improved payment and conditions for workers, and supported the economic policy of Fianna Fáil, seeing it as opening the way to badly needed employment. This last step provoked criticism from within the Jesuits, however, and a directive was issued that involvement in political matters was to be avoided. Indeed, Ryan was to earn a reputation among some of his fellow Jesuits, including later in China, as a zealous man of large ideas but questionable judgement, who sought to be involved in public issues but who was rather impractical in financial matters.

Mission to China

In 1932, far greater scope for his zeal, energy and ability opened up for the young priest. Some years earlier he had volunteered for the Irish Jesuit mission to China but had been turned down because of ill-health. By 1932, however, his health was no longer a concern. He volunteered again, and this time he was accepted.

Priests and nuns leaving for the missions in those years had no expectation of ever returning home, and Tom's departure was a severe blow to the people of Dublin's north inner-city. At a meeting at the Belvedere Newsboys Club, Tom was greatly moved by a gift from the boys of a chalice and paten, for which they had been saving from their meagre income for some time. There were further presentations from 'the poor people of the area' and from a troop of the Catholic Boy Scouts.

He left Ireland on 4 August 1933. The following day, the *Irish Independent* provided a vivid account of the scene before he departed. Under the heading, 'Jesuit leaves for China – Procession to Boat', the paper recorded:

> Fr Thomas Ryan SJ, who was the friend of Dublin's newsboys and all tenement dwellers in Dublin, left the city last night for the Chinese Mission. It was the occasion of a remarkable demonstration by the people amongst whom he had ministered for many years. For more than an hour before Fr Ryan left Belvedere College, crowds assembled in the vicinity ... hoping to get a glance of the priest whom they had known and loved so long.

As he got into the car taking him to the docks, a procession went ahead of it led by St Mary's Catholic Pipers. At the North Wall,

Scouts formed a guard of honour and saluted Fr Ryan as he stepped out of the car. He had to shake hands with scores of people before he was allowed to ascend the gangway to the S.O. *Lady Leinster*.

The scene at the quayside was the most remarkable witnessed for many years. Crowds surged around the gangway – many women with children in their arms – and, as the popular missionary made his way aboard, cried 'God Bless You Father Ryan'.

Among the newsboys present was a boy called Mutt. Exceptionally gifted as a whistler, it appears that Mutt could convincingly whistle Albert Katèlby's *In a Monastery Garden*, with all its complex ornamentation. One of the memories that Tom Ryan cherished to the end of his life was the sound of Mutt's whistling wafting across the waters as he paid farewell to his native land, as he believed, for the last time.

An Expanding Mission

Tom Ryan made the long, tedious journey to Hong Kong with four other Jesuits. They were aware that a great deal had already been achieved by the handful of men who had started the mission a mere seven years earlier. They had built and opened a university hostel, Ricci Hall. Some of them were lecturing in Hong Kong University. Others, at the request of the bishops of China and the bishop of Hong Kong, were active in running a seminary to train priests for the Chinese mission. A further episcopal request had led the Jesuits to assume editorship of the Catholic magazine, *The Rock*.

Most recently, in January 1933, the Irish Jesuits had taken over a successful secondary school, Wah Yan College, at the request of the school's founder. It was the largest secondary school for Chinese students in Hong Kong, with some 800 pupils and thirty teachers, and it was to prove a key centre of influence in the Irish mission.

Another initiative had a sad ending. Two Jesuits, who had been running a junior school in Canton at the bishop's request, died from cholera within a short time of their arrival. Their deaths had been on Tom's mind during his second request to be sent on the Chinese mission.

First Years in Hong Kong

On arrival in Hong Kong, the newcomers were warmly welcomed by their Jesuit colleagues, and then, after a few days, were despatched to locations in southern China to learn the language. Tom spent a year in Shiuhing, a city situated northeast of Hong Kong in Guangdong Province, before returning to Hong Kong, in 1934, to start teaching in Wah Yan College. There he eventually became the main English teacher to the senior classes. Years later, one of his former pupils recalled how well prepared his English classes were, and how interesting he made the poetry and literature he taught. Essays were returned quickly, carefully marked and with encouraging comments.

Characteristically, Tom also busied himself with social matters at the same time. In 1934, he enthused a group of university students at Ricci Hall into forming a social service club. The aim of the group was 'to stimulate sympathetic interest in the welfare of the less fortunate members of society and to encourage work for their assistance'. Tom told the students that they should consider themselves privileged to be in a position to serve those who were less well-off, and he outlined various ways they could do so. Encouraging them to study social problems, he also proposed that they undertake a social survey of Hong Kong. This need not be elaborately done, he pointed out, but would be a useful basis for helping others to work together for the good of all. He then provided specific headings for the survey, among them 'Housing', 'Public Health', 'Education', 'Recreation Areas' and 'Public Parks'.

At Wah Yan College, Tom encouraged a colleague, Fr Joe Howatson, to found the Shoeshiners' Club. Based on the pattern of the Belvedere Newsboys' Club, this blossomed into a large and very effective enterprise involving boys and girls. Outside the field of education, and through his social ministry, Ryan became friendly with the Anglican bishop of Hong Kong and Macao, Rt Revd Ronald Owen Hall. Together they founded the Hong Kong Housing Society, which pioneered the provision of low-cost housing and housing management. Eventually, this society would house over 100,000 people in about 20,000 flats in more than fourteen estates.

Several decades after his death, the name of Fr Thomas Ryan was still remembered, and an estate was named after him in the early years of the twenty-first century.

A year after his arrival back in Hong Kong, Ryan was appointed editor of *The Rock*, which appeared monthly. With his energy, social commitment, worldwide interests and fluent pen, the magazine flourished, its readership reaching far beyond Hong Kong itself. He continued as its editor until the Japanese invasion in 1941. At the same time, he became a popular radio presenter, giving regular talks on novelists, poets, dramatists and essayists, and also on art and music, painters and composers. In addition, he gave talks on directly religious matters, which proved very popular. His energy seemed endless, his work rate remarkable, and his range of knowledge extensive.

The Refugee Crisis

In 1938 the Japanese assault on Canton led to a flood of refugees into the Hong Kong territories. The government of Hong Kong approached Fr Ryan, asking him to take responsibility for the refugee camps, where some 50,000 people were expected. The camps operated under the direction of a refugee committee of four persons, one of whom was Ryan himself, while the government provided shelters, medical services, doctors, nurses and food. Fr Ryan was the chief organiser of these camps. His first camp, situated in a former airfield, catered for 5,000 refugees. As the need arose, he began to organise a second, and then a third camp, and thereafter he continued to expand the camps in the light of the demand.

At the end of November 1938, the Japanese advance came close to the British frontier, and within a few days between 40,000 and 50,000 people crossed into the British colony, seeking refuge. Faced with this overwhelming influx, Ryan approached the headmaster of Wah Yan College, Fr Daniel Donnelly SJ, requesting the assistance of the senior boys in the crisis. Responding positively, Donnelly brought two dozen boys to Fanling, an extensive location in an area rented from the Chinese known as the New Territories. The boys proved very effective. Communicating easily with the refugees in their own language, they dealt sympathetically with them, while organising them in a way that would not have occurred to Westerners. Their presence gave Frs Ryan and Donnelly the opportunity of travelling about the region collecting surplus clothing and food, and everything else that could be of use.

By January 1939, Ryan was able to report that his work was easing: the number of refugees was now down to 20,000, he had recently signed a contract for one hundred tons of rice per month, and he had a permanent staff in all the camps and food kitchens. His main task now was to organise life within the camps. In typical fashion, he set about providing schools for the children and work for the adults. Numerous industries were set up, catering for both male and female workers. The result was 'a wonderful spirit' in the camp. People were prepared to work for nothing, largely due, in Ryan's view, to the presence of more than a hundred volunteers. All of these were Chinese – 'for I will not accept any other help in the refugee camps,' he said – and were giving their time and services free for the benefit of their less fortunate countrymen.

The Japanese Attack and Aftermath

On 9 December 1941, two days after the attack on Pearl Harbour, Japanese planes bombed Hong Kong. The whole area also came under artillery fire and, although the siege was short, it was intense. Many people were killed and wounded, and there was much suffering and destruction of property. Fr Ryan and several other Jesuits became directly involved in assisting the auxiliary services, driving ambulances throughout the bombardment. Others remained active, to the extent that they could, in the seminary and in Wah Yan College. A second Wah Yan College, recently established in Kowloon, was obliged to close, although it later reopened. The experience of those days was vividly recorded in an account Ryan later put together at the request of his superior. This was subsequently published under the title, *Jesuits Under Fire in the Siege of Hong Kong*, and won favourable reviews in Britain, the United States and Ireland.

Early on, the Japanese made it clear that they were not going to feed the two million people who lived in the twin cities of Hong Kong and Kowloon. In the ensuing panic, people departed for the mainland in their thousands, many dying in the effort to reach their home villages. In response, some people – Ryan and a number of Jesuits among them – decided to travel to Free China, the region not occupied by Japanese or communists, to help with this new crisis.

Initially, Ryan settled in Kweilin in the Kwangsi province but, after it fell to the Japanese, he had to move Chunking, the capital of Free China. Soon he was appointed to take charge of all relief work for Catholics, and to be the Catholic representative in gatherings of other relief organisations. It was a vast undertaking, hugely demanding and involving much travel and diplomacy. He made such an impression, however, that a key British official invited him to London to join the planning group that was making arrangements for the post-war government of Hong Kong.

A New Challenge
Returning to Hong Kong, Ryan came face to face with the death, poverty and destruction suffered by the refugee population, and he and Fr Howatson set about doing what they could with slender resources. Meantime, Ryan was faced with a new challenge. A proposal had been made to the government to help the struggling farmers in the New Territories by taking charge of all wholesale marketing, and Ryan was asked to study the proposal and make a report. He did so, made his recommendations, and found himself unexpectedly invited to be the director of marketing. This was an entirely new venture for him, but he tackled it, as always, with gusto. He managed to get the necessary legislation passed, establishing a marketing organisation which bypassed the middle man and ensuring a better price for both farmer and the consumer. Ryan became, in effect, acting superintendent of agriculture, with a staff of two hundred people. He subsequently established something similar for the benefit of the Hong Kong fishermen, a cooperative which quickly flourished and continues to exist.

As a city man himself, Ryan knew little about farming or fishing, but he knew how to get reliable information and advice, and had the ability to get things done. His enthusiasm was infectious, and he was happy to delegate responsibility to people he had learned to trust. In this way, he managed to set up a pig-breeding station and several experimental farms, and eventually to get a department of agriculture established. In an imaginative move, he imported seedlings from Australia to compensate for the extensive destruction of trees by the Japanese. The fruit of this latter initiative can still be seen today in the plenitude of trees in Hong Kong and its surrounding areas.

The government wanted Ryan to stay on as a permanent official, but he had no wish for such a role. In the event, he was spared any pressure by being appointed superior of the Irish Jesuit Mission to Hong Kong and China in 1947.

Superior of the Mission

After the war years, it was widely felt that there was great scope for the advancement of the Jesuit Mission and that Fr Ryan, with his organising ability, his experience of dealing with Chinese people of every station, and his links with the Hong Kong government, was the best choice to lead the mission forward. As was to be expected, he brought new energy and ideas to the Jesuit mission in this role, sending young men abroad to be trained for work with the poor, with youth and in the field of industrial relations. In particular, he set his eyes on expanding the mission in Canton, hoping that some Jesuits would work in the university there. The Chinese mainland was in a troubled state at this time. A civil war was being waged between the communists from the north under Mao Zedong and the nationalist army of Chiang Kai-shek. The communists had met with much success, but no one seemed to think that Canton and southern China was in danger. Acting on this assumption, the new superior pressed ahead energetically with plans for the Canton area. All went well until early in 1949, when the communists advanced into south China. In April, Fr Ryan was forced to withdraw his men from Canton.

Ryan now had a surplus of active men in Hong Kong, some of them disheartened and restless. In addition, among the Jesuits in Wah Yan College, there was a sense of exhaustion. In an effort to meet the needs of the huge population, Fr Ryan had introduced a third school in addition to the two already in existence there, so that there were now three schools to be run: a day school, an afternoon school and a night school. Dissatisfaction took root, criticism of Fr Ryan's governance began to grow, and eventually a complaint was sent to Rome. In response, an official visitor was appointed, who found against Fr Ryan. As a consequence, Ryan was removed from office and replaced by one of his critics, whose style of governance turned out to be cautious and conservative. The vibrancy, excitement and colour generated by the Ryan years became a thing of the past. He, for his part, accepted his demotion without complaint, and always refused to talk about the person who, he knew, was mainly responsible for his downfall.

Concluding Years

In 1950, Fr Ryan went back to the classroom and to his radio talks on religion, art, music and opera, which he undertook with the same enthusiasm and commitment as he had always shown. He also wrote a number of historical works on the Church in Hong Kong and on the Jesuit connections with China from St Francis Xavier to the twentieth century.

Fr Ryan was greatly respected by the majority of his colleagues and greatly loved by his Chinese students, past and present. One former student, Maurice Lee Mui-Sang, recalled with affection, in 2010, the impact Fr Ryan had had on him during his student days in Wah Yan College:

> His way of teaching was unique and interesting. He would spend about ten minutes coaching us how to appreciate different kinds of architecture and painting before commencing the class. He would also invite us to go back to the school music room on Saturday evenings to enjoy

classical music, after which he would provide us with biscuits and hot drinks and chat with us like old friends.

Fr Ryan also made arrangements for us to be ushers when there was a famous orchestra performing in City Hall, so that we might have the chance to appreciate the world-class music and, at the same time, learn how to serve others. We really cherished these opportunities.

Fr Ryan would never refuse anyone approaching him after classes, and I often saw him sitting on the bench behind the Fathers' Chapel counselling the students. I can never forget what he taught me: 'What you dislike in another, take care to correct in yourself'. I can proudly say Fr Ryan cultivated in me the knowledge that I cannot learn elsewhere.

We loved him so much that we held a tea party to celebrate his seventy-second birthday in our classroom which was well decorated by us with crepe paper, ribbons and colourful balloons.

Fr Ryan surely appreciated that tea party. It was a heartfelt, if modest, tribute from his students to this much-loved man and his influence on their lives. It was another student, one who had become influential, who arranged a different kind of tribute to Fr Ryan: a plaque in St George's Royal Chapel, Windsor Castle. Together, these two tributes sum up the extraordinary contribution made by this humble Jesuit: teacher, writer, champion of the poor, pioneer of social reform, servant of the people – a man of God and a man for others.

PART THREE
Europe

~ 4 ~

A Giant of God:
Peter Kenney SJ (1779–1841)

Thomas J. Morrissey SJ

Introduction

It was inevitable that Pope Clement XIV (1705–1774) would find himself entangled in the political and religious turmoil that was engulfing Europe towards the end of the eighteenth century. Under mounting pressure from powerful countries – mainly France, Spain and Portugal – to abolish the Jesuits, the Pope eventually succumbed on 21 July 1773, with the publication of the Brief, *Dominus ac Redemptor.* The result was the almost total elimination of the Jesuits, their schools, churches and missions. Ironically, the sole defenders of the Jesuits were Catherine the Great of Russia and Frederick the Great of Prussia, leaders of Orthodox and Protestant states respectively, who both refused to promulgate the edict of suppression.

In the years following the suppression, before the Society was formally restored in 1814, many former Jesuits kept alive the hope that the order could be revived. They worked to boost the morale of their scattered companions, and prepared for the future by handing on the spirit of the Society to a growing number of young men who were awaiting its restoration. Among the latter group was Irishman, Peter Kenney, credited with restoring the Jesuits in

Ireland, but whose influence would reach far beyond the shores of his native land.

Early Life and Education

Peter James Kenney was born in Dublin on 7 July 1779. His father, also named Peter, and his mother Ellen, née Molloy, ran a small business in the city. Apart from Peter, the other known children were Anne Mary, who joined the Sisters of St Clare, and an older brother – or perhaps half-brother – Michael, who set up an apothecary shop in Waterford.

Apprenticed for a while to a coachbuilder, Peter owed his educational opportunities to a former Jesuit priest, Dr Thomas Betagh, who ran schools for poor children and apprentices in the cellars and backstreets of Dublin. Betagh also organised a classical school in the city, which Kenney later attended. Betagh made a huge impression on Kenney, as did another former Jesuit, Richard Callaghan, and they were both certainly instrumental in instilling in him a desire to follow their path as a Jesuit, should that prove possible.

Carlow, Stonyhurst and Sicily

The survival of the Jesuits in White Russia – roughly the equivalent of today's Belarus – was the consequence of Catherine the Great's decision not to promulgate the brief of suppression in her territories. When that situation was formally recognised by the papacy in 1801, hopes rose for a general restoration of the order. As a result, that same year Fr Callaghan sent Kenney and some other students of Betagh, who were hoping to join a restored Society of Jesus, to Carlow College to prepare for the priesthood. From there they were sent to Stonyhurst College in Lancashire, run by former English Jesuits, where they commenced their novitiate in 1804. From the beginning of his time there, Kenney impressed staff and students alike with his evident ability, sound piety and eloquence. Concerns about his health arose, however – he suffered from asthma all his life – and it was these concerns that prompted his transfer to Sicily in 1808, where the Society had been formally reinstated four years earlier.

At that time, the island of Sicily was in danger of invasion by Napoleon, and was dependent on the British navy and military garrison for its defence. For this reason, Kenney's ordination, along with that of his colleagues, was brought forward, so that he was ordained on 4 December 1808. Remaining in Sicily until 1811, Kenney found himself captivated by the island's rich cultural and historical tradition, leading to a deepening of his own cultural and spiritual sensibilities. As earlier in Stonyhurst, Kenney made a deep impression on his colleagues and superiors in Sicily. Indeed, his ability and general maturity so impressed his Jesuit superior that he termed him *'L'incomparable P. Kenney'*.

During his time in Sicily, Kenney was chosen to act as interpreter in a British naval expedition to rescue the pope from imprisonment by Napoleon. As it happened, the pope refused to leave Rome, and the expedition came to nothing. Kenney and an English Jesuit friend, Thomas Glover, also acted as chaplains to Catholic soldiers and sailors in the British forces on the island, many of whom were Irish. Their efforts were terminated by the intolerance of those they termed 'Scotch generals'. Kenney and Glover sent a report to London about this matter, which gave rise to questions in the House of Commons.

Return to Ireland

When Kenney returned to Ireland on 31 August 1811, he must have been greatly saddened by the absence of his friend and mentor, Thomas Betagh, who had died a few months earlier. Betagh had followed the career of his favourite pupil with great interest, speaking to his colleagues in the diocese about Kenney's remarkable gifts and attainments. Acting on Betagh's judgement, the coadjutor archbishop of Dublin, Dr Daniel Murray – who, like Kenney, was a former student of Betagh – quickly sought Kenney's assistance in dealing with a major challenge he was facing in Maynooth College, the national seminary.

Serious problems of morale and discipline had arisen in the college, and Murray invited Kenney to join him in addressing the situation. Within a year, with Murray as president and Kenney as vice-president, morale was restored and the college was transformed. Kenney's sermons and spiritual meditations had a profound impact on the students, many of whom wrote them down, so that they were passed on to other students for years to come.

The Founding of Clongowes

By the early years of the nineteenth century, the situation in Europe had changed radically, and in August 1814 Pope Pius VII announced the universal restoration of the Society of Jesus. Anticipating that event by several months, Kenney moved quickly. He availed of the money that had been saved by former Irish Jesuits against the day the Society would be restored, and set about buying a large property in a quiet area of County Kildare, with the intention of founding a secondary school for boys. His hopes were that, with the anticipated coming of emancipation for Catholics, the school would be instrumental in educating a future Catholic leadership. Clongowes Wood College, as it was called, became indeed the leading boarding school for middle-class Catholic boys in Ireland.

Kenney was convinced that a good beginning was essential for the project, and he must have been satisfied when 110 pupils were enrolled in the school's first year. That number rose to a remarkable 200 students in the following year, with the result that many of them had to be lodged in improvised accommodation. As well as being rector and headmaster, Kenney was appointed the first superior of the Irish mission. This was a particularly taxing role in this time of transition, the demands of which meant that he frequently had to be away from Clongowes. He had a gift for detailed organisation, however, and the college ran successfully under delegated authority. It helped that the structures he established in Clongowes were similar to those he had experienced in Stonyhurst and in the Royal College in Palermo. On most Sundays he was present himself to address the school, enthusing his hearers with his vision of Christian values, and conveying to them the high standards of life, work and discipline he expected from a Clongowes boy.

Word of Kenney's commitment to his students, his assured manner, his organisational ability, and his sheer energy spread abroad, attracting prospective parents who valued the firm, yet relaxed, discipline he engendered. Mary O'Connell, wife of Daniel O'Connell, probably spoke for many others when she mentioned the contentment of their sons in Clongowes under Kenney, who 'seemed to be more of a kind parent than anything else to them'. Kenney kept the students' fathers informed of their sons' progress using diplomatic, yet forthright, words.

Further Initiatives in Ireland

Not content with developing a major school in trying circumstances, Kenney, between the years 1814 and 1819, became involved in several other initiatives. He started a novitiate near Tullamore, in the Irish midlands, which later became St Stanislaus College, and he opened a small church and residence at Hardwicke Street in Dublin, which subsequently blossomed into St Francis Xavier's Church in Gardiner Street and nearby Belvedere College. As well as giving numerous retreats to priests and religious and delivering many public sermons, Kenney also served as adviser to three new religious congregations: the Irish Christian Brothers, the Irish Sisters of Charity and the Sisters of Loreto, and assisted them in drawing up their constitutions.

Despite all the marks of success, however, critical murmurs began to emerge from his community in Clongowes. Some of them considered him too ascetic, too strict. Two members wrote to Rome in complaint, and an official visitor was sent who found against Kenney. As a consequence, in 1817, Kenney was replaced by Fr Charles Aylmer, one of his critics. Before leaving Clongowes, Kenney went on his knees before the community to ask their pardon for any hurt he might have caused during his time as rector. While this gesture may seem somewhat baroque to us today, the sight of this great man asking forgiveness had a profound effect on some of the younger members of the community. It is surely a measure of his humility.

Kenney was not long back in the ranks before word came, in 1819, that the Superior General of the Society had further need of his advice and skills. He wished him to go as his representative to the United States of America.

First Visit to the American Mission

Kenney's task, as the general outlined it, was an important and daunting one. First of all, he was to report on and deal with the serious divisions that were said to exist between 'native American' and 'foreign' Jesuits; secondly, he was to report on the condition of the farms which helped to finance the Society's works and which were said to be in a state of disorder, and to suggest ways of improving them; finally, he was to examine the situation of Georgetown University, then in very distressed condition, and suggest appropriate remedies.

Kenney's letters from the New World suggest that in many ways he lost his heart to the United States and its possibilities. Indeed, always after his return he would keep in touch with developments there. The letters he sent to Rome cover a wide range of issues: the spirit of independence he found among native-born Jesuits, and their need for discipline; clashes between Church authorities and lay trustees; the question of slavery and its complexities. He also mentions the political system in operation in the United States, and the possibilities it could open up for the Church and the formerly oppressed peoples of Europe, especially his own countrymen.

As the general's representative, he exercised his authority by introducing regulations regarding the administration of the mission, the position of the slaves, and financial control. The structures of Georgetown University were modified, and its position was temporarily stabilised. In a significant move, he decided to send six young men to Rome for training who, on their return, would prove to be effective presidents for the university and solid leadership for the mission and future province.

Kenney made a favourable impression on bishops and diocesan clergy as well as on his fellow Jesuits. Indeed, some prelates were sufficiently impressed to put forward his name, at different times, for the bishoprics of Cincinnati, New York and Philadelphia. It was the strong possibility of the latter appointment, which was being considered during the interregnum following the death of the Jesuit general, that led him to hurry back to Europe in 1820. In Rome, he attended the General Congregation convoked to elect a new superior general, reported on American affairs as he found them and made a strong plea for the mission. He also made a noteworthy intervention in support of classical education and the traditional Jesuit approach to education as outlined in the *Ratio Studiorum*.

Returning to Ireland in 1821, Kenney found that his name had been put forward for the dioceses of both Kerry and Armagh. In the event, he was made superior of the Irish mission once more, and soon found himself in constant demand for retreats and special sermons throughout the country.

The death of the Jesuit general, Aloysius Fortis, in 1829, meant another General Congregation was called to elect his successor. Kenney's attendance at it was marked by a powerful and decisive intervention on behalf of the theology of St Thomas Aquinas, and also by the elevation of the Irish mission to the status of a vice-province. His intervention made a deep impression on the new Fr General, John Roothaan, who had a special interest in the American mission and hoped to raise it to the status of a province of the Society.

Second Visit to the United States

To that end, Roothaan decided to send Kenney to the United States once more, this time both as visitor and overall superior. Kenney was loath to go at first. His enthusiasm for the American mission had been weakened by the chronic asthma he suffered and by his ageing and overweight body. He overcame his reluctance, however, by his wish to be detached from his own concerns and by his commitment to religious obedience.

During the years 1830 to 1834 Kenney was greatly taken up with American affairs. First he spent time in Maryland – in Georgetown, Frederick, and the various farms or 'missions' in that region. Then he travelled to Missouri, a distance of well over 1,000 kilometres, where he helped to strengthen the university foundation at St Louis, bring order into the Jesuit finances there, and establish priorities in the face of the numerous demands for Jesuit services. Rules were drawn up to address various issues that needed attention: community living, positions of leadership and responsibility, the delegation of authority, the running of farms, and the controversial question of the slaves and their treatment. Kenney emphasised the commitment of the Missouri mission to the indigenous population, and the letters he wrote from St Louis reveal something of that city's position as gateway to the west. He kept a journal of his travels, offering fascinating insights into the social life and developments of the time, as well as providing descriptions of the rivers, towns and customs he encountered.

Eventually, before returning to Ireland, Kenney announced the establishment of Maryland as a province of the Society of Jesus, and the Missouri region as a separate mission reporting directly to the general. As Kenney left North America for the last time, he was held in high esteem by the bishops, clergy and laity who had met him, but above all by his fellow Jesuits. 'Never has a man lived among us', reads the diary of Georgetown University, 'whom all without exception so loved and reverenced.' Seventy years later, a Jesuit historian of the Maryland province, E. J. Devitt, was moved to write in almost excessively eulogistic terms of Kenney's first and second visitations:

> Rarely indeed were such talents as were his united in one person … Vision, courage, confidence in God, utter abandonment to the lead of obedience, these made Peter Kenney a man almost beyond compare in this country. Apparently he could not be frightened … It was a gigantic undertaking, and only a giant of God with the spirit of a child could bring it to the crown of success.

Final years

For this tired man, who was growing corpulent and increasingly short of breath, the transition from the vast horizons of North America to the smaller but intense world of Dublin – with its teeming population, poverty, deep faith and incessant demands – was itself a major challenge. Nevertheless, he was asked to be superior of the vice-province as well as superior of the busy Gardiner Street Church community. It proved too much for him. Snowed under with work, he was unable to find time to send the expected reports to Rome about the vice-province, and eventually the general removed him from that position, much to his relief.

From then on, Kenney devoted all the energy he had left in serving people from all walks of life, spending long hours in the confessional. His capacity to be all things to all people, his compassion and empathy, his common touch – these meant that he could be equally at home with sailors, cabbies and labourers as with the professional and commercial classes. His work in those years earned him the title among his contemporaries, 'the modern apostle of Dublin ... and of Ireland at large'.

His health, which had never been robust, declined noticeably under the cumulative pressures of the demands made on him. Lack of exercise contributed to his corpulence, asthma left him stooped, and he aged perceptibly. To Archbishop Ullathorne of Birmingham, who visited Dublin between 1836 and 1838, Kenney seemed 'advanced in years' although, in fact, he was only in his late fifties.

Despite his declining health, Kenney's colleagues chose him to represent them at the Congregation of Jesuit Procurators in 1841, held in Rome to evaluate the state of the Society. He set out in October, but his journey was beset with floods, delays and unexpected hardships. Exhausted by the time he reached Rome, he had to be carried up the stairs to attend the congregation's meetings. Unable to recover his strength, he was eventually struck down by a stroke. The doctor who was called suggested bleeding him to relieve the pressure, but Kenney let it be known that his own doctor in Ireland had counselled against such a course, believing it would be likely to prove fatal. Fr General, when consulted, suggested that a second opinion should be sought. When the second doctor also recommended bleeding, Kenney acquiesced. He was dead within a few hours.

Fr General Roothaan and most members of the congregation were present at his bedside as Kenney passed away. By special permission of the general, he was interred with the Jesuit generals under the main altar of the Church of the Gesù, the principal Jesuit Church in Rome. He was sixty-two years of age.

When the news of his death reached Ireland there was intense anguish on the part of Kenney's many friends. Mary Aikenhead, founder of the Irish Sisters of Charity, felt ill on hearing the news. Archbishop Murray cancelled his engagements, observing that Rome was 'the only spot that was worthy of his death-place'. These words reflect the fact that Kenney was a man of the entire Church whose interests, far from being confined to Ireland, included North America and Britain, and beyond to India, Australia, New Zealand and South America.

His burial place in the Gesù was also an acknowledgement that he was a man of the world-wide Society of Jesus, who had influenced its fortunes across the globe. His journey, from the damp cellars of Penal Dublin to the vaults of the Gesù, had been a long and testing one, and it was fitting that he should find his final resting place in the Eternal City. His journey's end was, in a special way, a homecoming.

~ 5 ~
Brother Courtesy:
Francisco Gárate SJ (1857–1929)

Errol Fernandes SJ

Francisco Gárate Aranguren was born in the Basque Country in the north of Spain in 1857, the second of seven brothers. His modest home was located a short distance from the castle where St Ignatius Loyola, the founder of the Jesuits, was born. Ignatius's birthplace is now the site of an impressive basilica, and it was there that Francisco regularly attended Mass. From a humble farming background, Francisco grew up in an atmosphere of faith and piety, but only received a few years of elementary education.

Early Years as a Jesuit
At the age of fourteen Francisco left home to undertake domestic work in a college that had been newly opened by the Jesuits in Orduña, not far from Bilbao. We don't know when he began to consider joining the Jesuits himself, but in 1874 he applied to be accepted as a brother in the Society of Jesus. Because of the unfavourable political situation in his own country, Francisco could not make his noviceship in Spain. Instead, he was directed to the novitiate in Poyanne, across the border in southwest France. Along with two companions, he undertook the 230 kilometres journey

before arriving in his new home to begin the first stage of his life as a Jesuit.

From his earliest days as a novice, his companions became aware of Francisco's prayerful life, his unassuming humility and his hard work. Many of them were inspired by his Spartan practices, trying to imitate his austere lifestyle and his attention to the detailed rules and regulations of the novitiate. The two years that he spent in the novitiate prepared him well for his future life of selfless service.

Francisco Gárate pronounced his first vows – which were also perpetual – in 1876, and his initial assignment was to the La Guardia College in Pontevedra, in the northwest of Spain, where he was appointed sacristan and infirmarian. He spent a little over a decade there, and such was his impact that many who had been sick in his care remembered their time in the infirmary with great affection. His reputation spread quickly throughout the college, with many of the students attributing their speedy recovery to the tender care of Brother Gárate.

Forty-One Years as Doorkeeper

In March 1888, Gárate was assigned as doorkeeper and sacristan to Deusto College in Bilbao, a university that had been opened by the Jesuits just two years earlier. Here he remained for the rest of his life, until his death in 1929. Many people probably thought that his position as sacristan and doorkeeper was of little significance in the life this burgeoning university, with its learned professors and ambitious students, but that was far from the reality.

As doorkeeper, Gárate was particularly well-placed to make an impression on everyone he greeted: lecturers, students, parents and visitors. In the performance of his duties, he distinguished himself by his serenity, discretion, humility, detachment and union with God. With his ability to welcome everyone warmly and with his negotiating skills, he earned himself the nickname 'Brother Courtesy', which proved to be singularly appropriate. He offered words of encouragement and helpful advice to countless students and was especially concerned with anyone in trouble of any kind.

In particular, he tended to students who were ill with great care and kindness.

Whenever the doorbell rang, Gárate would respond with the words, 'Yes Lord, I am coming', and he would greet each visitor with the respect borne of that faith. Legend has it that on one occasion when he answered the door, Our Lord and his Blessed Mother did appear before him. Gárate was not surprised, the story goes, because he had learned to see his Lord present in everyone who crossed his path. He had learned, as a true follower of St Ignatius, to find God in all things and all things in God. His job as doorkeeper was not a chore or a job, but a vocation within his vocation as a Jesuit.

Professors, students, parents, workmen – they all came to Gárate to share their concerns, and he reached out to them all. Though he did not have any academic degrees, those who approached him could see that he had a wisdom that did not come from books or formal qualifications. His wisdom came from a deeper place. It was a practical wisdom that he learned from his close contact with God and his concern for people from every background. Gárate was always willing to share this wisdom with those who were open to it. He was selfless in everything.

Prayer and Action Together
People remarked how simply Gárate lived his personal life. His room was unadorned, his clothes clean but well worn, his meals frugal. It was clear to everyone that there was no dichotomy between prayer and action in his life. While there was no doubt that he was a prayerful man – he was always seen with his rosary beads in his hands – he translated the consolations that he received in prayer into action. Available and ready to help everyone who came to him, at whatever time, his life was a lived prayer.

His patience was endless, no matter how great the demands made on him. The entrance hall where he was stationed was a place of ceaseless activity – parents coming to meet their children, visitors asking to see the fathers or professors, tradespeople delivering their goods, beggars asking for alms – and for everyone Brother Gárate had a courteous and friendly word, spoken with remarkable serenity and calm. When he was asked how he was able to remain so calm in the middle of all these demands, he replied simply, 'I do what I can and leave the rest to God who can do everything. With his help, all is easy and pleasant because we serve a good Master'. This indeed was the secret of his serenity, and of his life.

There was nothing remarkable about Brother Gárate's outward appearance, and there are no exciting stories to be told about him. He has no great achievements to his name that will be recorded in the history books. What touched the people who met him was something deeper and more mysterious: a quality of graciousness that was rare and a holiness that radiated from his person. It was enough for people to exchange words with him, even for a short time, to realise that he was a man of deep spirituality who lived out of an inner serenity.

Gárate saw himself as a servant in the vineyard of the Lord, and lived out this conviction in his ordinary, humdrum life. He took seriously the saying of Jesus, 'When you have done all that you were ordered to do, say, "We are useless sevants; we have done no more than our duty"' (Lk 17:10). For Gárate, it was a privilege to serve in the vineyard of the Lord, and the serving was already his reward. This conviction consumed him so completely that he could go on and on without tiring or giving up. It sustained him to the very end. In this he was the embodiment of what St Ignatius calls 'indifference' in the *Spiritual Exercises*. 'Indifference' in this context means freedom, and Gárate was profoundly free: he was detached from the outcome of his own actions because he was totally consumed with concern for the other.

Gracious to the End

Gárate's health started to fail in early September 1929, and one day, after Mass, he began to suffer sharp abdominal pains. He reluctantly agreed to remain in bed, and later that evening he asked to be anointed. His discomfort increased, and a nurse called the doctor, who decided to operate on his blocked urethra. That gave him some relief, but despite the successful operation his health continued to decline.

True to his convictions, Gárate was gracious and positive to the end. He was aware that he was in God's hands and the pain and discomfort did not seem to affect his demeanour. He had learned to place himself in the hands of the Lord he so trusted, and he was confident that all that was happening was in God's care and would be for God's greater glory. Like Jesus, he was able to commend his spirit into the hands of the Lord (Lk 23:46), knowing full well that God was gracious and full of kindness, waiting to greet him at the door of another, much greater mansion.

Brother Gárate died on 9 September 1929. Interestingly, that day was the feast of another Jesuit, St Peter Claver, who had himself been inspired by a Jesuit brother, St Alphonsus Rodriguez (1532–1617). Gárate's life resembles that of Alphonsus in many ways. Like Gárate, Alphonsus spent his Jesuit life as a doorkeeper, working for forty-five years in the Jesuit college in Majorca. Like Gárate three centuries later, Alphonsus brought consolation and hope to teachers, students and visitors alike with his faith-filled presence and words of wisdom. Like Gárate, he had a wisdom born of prayer and service.

At Gárate's funeral, many people could be seen placing their rosaries and crucifixes on his coffin, asking for his prayers and support. His remains were initially buried in the local cemetery, but were later transferred – as was only right – to the University of Deusto, where they were placed in the pavement of its public chapel. Time went by, but his holiness was not forgotten. Demands for his beatification became persistent, and eventually the formal process got under way. Beginning in December 1939 and continuing until the end of July 1940, all the available documentation about his life was collated and the testimony of witnesses to his saintliness recorded. He was beatified by Pope St John Paul II on 6 October 1985.

An Enduring Inspiration
Because of his single-minded focus and unwavering fidelity, Francisco Garáte's life and can be an inspiration for all of us. He

learned the art of living fully every moment of the day. He was able to do the most ordinary things with extraordinary love, kindness and generosity. He lived his life in a positive and affirmative frame of mind, confident of God's presence in all circumstances. His life is a reminder to us of what is truly important in life: not so much the external work we do or the achievements we claim, as the attitude we take to what we do and the people we meet. Brother Courtesy directs our gaze to the deeper realities we are all called to embody.

~ 6 ~

Greatness of Soul:
John Hyde SJ (1910–1985)

Patrick Gallagher

I can see him still, a small man about five feet four inches in height, of trim build. In general, his eyes are cast down but he is keenly aware of what matters in his surroundings. He is dressed in a black clerical suit, a black hat and a roman collar. When on his bike his trousers are protected with bicycle clips that reveal his black well-kept boots. The bike itself is in sound shape. It is an all-steel machine with just the basics. The handlebars are of the old north road raised type. He is moving unobtrusively along the back roads of Rahan in the Irish rural midlands and, later in life, on the busy roads of a Dublin suburb.

Who was this man who was so self-effacing that he could easily be overlooked or forgotten? John Hyde was his name, a Jesuit, a priest, a lover of the poor and sick, an outstanding philosopher and a profound theologian.

A Unique Personality

John's room tells us a lot about him. The plain, wooden table, the kneeler at which he prayed, the simple but tidy bed were the main objects in it. There was an armchair but I never saw him sitting in it. It was for others to sit in. His watch was on the table beside the bookstand. Only those books in regular use were in the room and they were few in number. Otherwise, an old typewriter, a pen, a small amount of paper. That was about it. I never saw into his clothes closet. I bet there was little in there.

Many students went to his room for help with their studies or spiritual life, and their stories reveal his inimitable character and his unique sense of humour. One Jesuit student from the continent went to him for help and he sat down waiting for John to speak. He did not know John's ways. A long time passed and eventually a knock came to the door. John simply said, 'I think we are being interrupted'.

Another time on a remote road in Rahan, a village near Tulla-more, County Offaly, John was on his bike heading for the Jesuit philosophate trying not to be late for dinner. A local with car trouble stopped him. Knowing Fr Hyde's reputation, he insisted he bless the car. Reluctantly, John did so and the darned car started. When he got back to the refectory he was asked why he was late. With a coy smile he simply said, 'I was working miracles'.

On another occasion, when a recent film by Pier Paulo Pasolini, *The Gospel According to St Matthew*, was being discussed at table, a member of the community turned to John, who had been silent up to that point, and asked him if he had seen the film. 'No,' was the reply, 'but I've read the book.'

John was a deep one, and sometimes he could be off-putting. He was quiet and would not in any way stand out. To some extent this was due to his growing up in Ballycotton, County Cork, in the early 1900s. It was a small fishing village then and bilingual in Irish and English. But his manner was much more an expression of the inner man. His humour came from a joy and kindness that shone through his twinkling eyes and gentle smile. It was his depth that grounded an extraordinary combination of qualities that enriched those who met him in varied circumstances. A word on some of these qualities.

Personal Qualities

There was a reverence about John that was otherworldly and yet it greatly enriched this world too. To see him praying slowed one down and encouraged a person to get in touch with another side of themselves. His composed interior and exterior helped him to be a very good listener, and many people sought his advice because of this. The advice would come from one who was in no way self-centred. If he did know, he told you that. If he wasn't sure, he told you that, too. If he thought he knew, he gave it as his opinion. This inner quietness seemed to communicate itself especially to distressed people, and helped calm them. John could just sit silently with them. His presence at the Knock shrine in County Mayo proved very consoling for very many people.

His inner composure also helped him to think and read, in other words to study. It came naturally to him. This orientation reflected what Aristotle called wonder, and it encouraged John to be a close observer of human nature and the world around him. From this he could readily draw amazingly helpful images in which an eager student could understand reality in all its complexity and richness. John used these images because he considered them central to the way we humans understand.

We have made some headway in our task of understanding John but before venturing out into deeper waters a few words are needed on why he did not make use of the media and electronic devices. Many are in the position of being too old to master this new way of living, and to some extent I include myself in this group. Certainly John was in it.

One cannot conclude from this, however, that he was out of touch. John reached many people at a different level altogether in a really vital way, just as many today are reaching other people through the media and electronics. Indeed the goal of this article is to put its readers in touch with that deeper level of the person named John Hyde because there is something really worthwhile down there. This is what we are now moving into, and we will strive to identify interlocking themes in his life.

Reverence and Magnanimity

Reverence is clearly one of these themes. Our question now is: what was the ultimate root of this in John's life? If we go back to Ballycotton we find that a sense of real dependence on the creator of this world and everyone in it pervaded the culture of the whole area; it was in the area's songs, in the work, in farming and fishing, in Sunday Mass, in personal prayers, in everything. It did not mean they were all living this belief. Often it just meant, at the least, that the creator was real, like everything else.

We know that John had this sense because of his real dependence on God. He was moved to put his whole life on the line and enter the Jesuits in Rahan in 1927. It was very definitely a defining moment in his life. Early in his noviceship John, along with the other novices, made the Spiritual Exercises of St Ignatius in silent retreat over thirty days. In the introductory material of the *Spiritual Exercises* Ignatius advises that a person should 'enter upon them with a large heart and liberality towards his Creator and Lord'. John was whole-hearted in all he did so we can be sure this deeply resonated with him. He knew some ten languages, and Spanish was one of them. It should not surprise us, then, to find out that later in life he would memorise the little book in its entirety in the original Spanish, so great was its influence on him.

The above advice would stand him well when he came to a reflection in the Exercises called the 'First Principle and Foundation'. We can well imagine the eighteen-year-old novice using the two complementary gifts of faith and reason on the great truths of God our creator and his plan for the whole of creation. John's sense of reverence is now firmly cemented in his whole make-up. To jump ahead in John's life, his superiors knew John well and saw in him a completely natural philosopher and theologian, so they saw to it that he was fully equipped for the task.

John spent his whole life trying to understand the wonderful life growing within him: reverence, a generous heart and now magnanimity. As far as I can see, he learned about the central role of magnanimity – 'greatness of soul' is a better translation – from three major influences in his life: Aristotle, Aquinas and Ignatius. It is explicit in Aristotle in his *Ethics* and in Aquinas in his *Summa*. It is there in Ignatius in at least two of his writings: in the *Exercises* themselves and, significantly, in part nine of the Jesuit *Constitutions*, where Ignatius is dealing with the qualities expected of a general of the Society of Jesus. A close reading of this text will bring handsome rewards.

Magnanimity urges us to undertake great things, and that is why Ignatius found it shed much light on his own constant reaching for the greatest good in life. The difficulty is that we are easily distracted, be it by ourselves or by what John called in Irish *saol*, meaning 'life' or 'the world'. Aristotle was very practical, and when writing on magnanimity he spoke perceptively of being at the bottom of the wheel of fortune when the greatest good in life looks hopelessly distant and finally disappears from your life. That is when magnanimity is essential. One has to reach deeply into one's soul to access the hope, courage and fortitude to respond to this challenge. It is why the Latin and Greek words for magnanimity are better translated by 'great souled'.

It is no wonder that Aristotle called magnanimity the crown of the virtues, because it, as it were, energises them and renders them actually effective in helping us bear the really big problems in our life. All of us need it, because who has not had a turn or two on the wheel of fortune and got lost and confused? When John was lecturing on philosophy in Rahan he focused on God as creator and our extraordinary relation of complete dependence on God that goes with this.

The philosophate in Rahan was closed in 1962 and John was moved to Milltown Park in Dublin to teach theology. It was truly an inspired appointment and he left his mark on every course he taught. As far as I know, it was now that he put into written form the combination of not just reverence and magnanimity, but also friendship with God that crowned his life and thought.

The Centrality of Friendship

Let us look at what he has to say about friendship, always keeping in mind that for John such intellectual reflection is on his own rich experience of these things, a reflection that naturally results in a further enriching of his basic experience. Friendship underlies such names as 'People of God' and 'Kingdom of God'. It was how the early Christians saw each other, and they called it in Greek *koinonia* or community.

Jesus called us friends, and Ignatius saw himself as founding a group called the Companions of Jesus. No less than Aristotle and Aquinas added their contribution, so it is clear that John is on to something very substantial and very significant. In what follows I will have to be selective and I will be working from John's own notes.

Friendship, John taught, can only come about between good persons. It is freely entered into and slowly becomes a habit in the technical sense of that word. A habit in this sense is the very opposite of a mechanical action, because it enables a person to do something good that is highly desirable, yet difficult, with relative ease and regularity. That is why friendship is very stable and friends can really depend on each other. If it is a serious friendship it involves them to their very depths, and it causes a wonderful change or development in each of them. People can see it in them through all they say and do, particularly in important matters involving choices. They see friends gladly communicating and sharing with each other, and they often wonder what that is. The fact is that the friends each wish the same fundamental good for each other.

This last point is so vital that living without friendship is very difficult. That is precisely why John saw it as naturally creating community, where community means sharing and communicating so that all concerned benefit from it. At a very early stage, this was locked into no less than our Creed, when we profess to believe in the communion of saints (with a small s). It is often overlooked, because we tend to think of friendship as between two persons, or a few at most. It definitely includes this but potentially includes all persons. Indeed, it is what drives the movement for social justice that is one of the finest developments of our times.

John himself asks himself a central question about human friendship as he comes closer to the theme of friendship with God: what is the truly one good that friends wish for each other? He replies, happiness. No one will normally deny that, but unfortunately there is much confusion regarding what makes us happy. John, then, is quietly courageous when he says that our happiness lies in being with God and – the addition is important – all that he has to give us of himself. He singles out the main thing in that 'all', and it is no less than God's own joy.

From Scripture we learn that the Father asked his Son to come and help us. The Son came willingly despite what lay ahead. Now we can see God as our friend in God made visible, namely Jesus. At the Last Supper, Jesus says to us, 'These things I have spoken to you, that my joy may be in you, and that your joy may be full' (Jn 15:11). This is exactly how friends speak to each other when sharing what means most to them.

In one of his articles in Irish John has this wonderful phrase, *'Is dual do Dhia áthas'*, meaning joy is natural to God or joy is in God's nature. It is precisely this joy that is the truly one good that God shares with us, and it was embedded in John's composed demeanour, his already mentioned smile and his attentive manner when listening. I think this all came from his inner joy.

Joy and Suffering

How did John handle the conflict between joy and all the sadness and despair that goes with the wheel of fortune mentioned earlier when reflecting on magnanimity? The question is nearly as hard to deal with as the unavoidable wheel of fortune itself. I want to ask this question because John asked it of himself, in his notes.

First, when Jesus was at the Last Supper and spoke of his joy, he clearly was aware of much that lay ahead that was not good. The joy, then, he is speaking of is no otherworldly joy in the sense of being unrealistic in a serious situation. John himself speaks of Jesus on the cross as never being so active even though he seems to be a victim. I think most of us know of a dreadful situation we were in that seemed to completely overpower us. What has John to say that can help us here? He speaks of patience and, although it suggests passivity, John sees that there is more to it than that.

That is why John says that, when we suffer innocently, we are not passive, but active; my own term for his insight is 'creative patience', because it tends to transform those confronted with it. This is exactly what was meant earlier when we said friendship creates community even in tough situations. It is this communication of goodness that, quietly but powerfully, through the personal communication of God as our friend, turns what looks like a lost cause into a new but wonderful joy.

Sharing his Joy

As I look back on John's life I see that a really hard-won sense of God's own joy was his in plenty, because they both talked together a lot and shared all they had with each other. He shared this same joy in his teaching and in helping others in their problems. Truly he showed reverence, generosity, magnanimity, friendship and creative patience as he went about it all.

I realise that I have touched on only a few of the central thoughts of his teaching and life. There is so much more. Shortly before he died he told me how he felt he was only beginning to appreciate the wonder, joy and beauty of our faith. I know he is now in the full presence of his best friend, God, sharing their joy.

~ 7 ~

A Life that Makes Sense:
John Sullivan SJ (1861–1933)

John Looby SJ

Nobody could have anticipated how John Sullivan's life would unfold. Born into a wealthy, privileged family, he was expected to follow in his father's footsteps in the legal profession. Instead, after much struggle and hesitation, he joined the Jesuits and came to be revered as an apostle of the poor and infirm, ready to cycle long distances to comfort anyone who sought his presence, and living a life of frugality and simplicity. The life of John Sullivan would make no sense if God did not exist.

A Privileged Background

John was the fourth and youngest son of Sir Edward Sullivan, whose distinguished legal career culminated in his becoming lord chancellor of Ireland in 1883. Shortly after John's birth in 1861, the family moved to Fitzwilliam Place in the south of the city. This was part of a prestigious area of elegant Georgian mansions, with a spacious park at the centre of the nearby square. It was to be home to John until he joined the Jesuits in 1900, when he was almost forty.

John's mother, Elizabeth Baily, was from Passage West in County Cork. Unlike her husband, who belonged to the Church of Ireland, she was a Catholic. In keeping with the custom of the time, the four sons, John included, were brought up in the father's Church, while the only daughter was reared a Catholic. The Sullivans provided an idyllic environment for the children, for they were happy together, and the children had the security of knowing they were greatly loved.

Sir Edward took great care with the children's education. He wanted his sons to be well educated gentlemen, qualified to practise law but well positioned should they choose another career. John followed his brothers to Portora Royal School in Enniskillen, County Fermanagh, reputedly the best Protestant school in Ireland, where he had great academic success as a gold medallist. He later went to Trinity College in Dublin, where he studied classics and law, and was similarly successful.

An Unsettled Period

When John was in the final stages of his legal studies, in 1885, his father died suddenly. This seems to have had an unsettling effect on him, because at that stage he abruptly left Trinity and headed for London, where he continued his legal studies and qualified for the English Bar in 1888. It seems, however, that the legal profession had lost its appeal for him, for he never did practise as a lawyer.

Instead, he began to travel in Europe, particularly in those lands associated with the Greek classics which he had earlier studied enthusiastically and loved deeply. He was an inveterate walker who enjoyed plunging into the icy-cold Alpine waters to refresh himself. People who met him at this time always mention his generosity. One acquaintance, who arrived in St Moritz shortly after John himself had come from a lengthy trek, tells how John promptly invited him to dinner in an expensive restaurant.

During his travels in Greece, John discovered the Orthodox monasteries on Mount Athos, and to these he returned again and again, at one stage spending some three months there during the Lenten season. It is now apparent that John's period of wandering was really a time of searching. He was searching how best to respond to God's call, a call to leave his own familiar place and to go, like

Abraham, into the land that God would show him. This part of his search finally ended on 21 December 1896, when he was received into the Catholic Church in the Jesuit church in Farm Street, London.

A New Beginning

On 7 September 1900, now almost forty years of age, John Sullivan finally left his home and made a new beginning; he entered the Jesuit noviciate in Rahan, near Tullamore in County Offaly. It was almost fifteen years since the death of his father, the event that had so unsettled him, and he now believed that he had found what God wanted him to do. He was following in the footsteps of Peter – and countless others after him – who responded to Jesus' call, 'Come, follow me'. Many years earlier, as a schoolboy in Portora, John had been moved by the words of St Paul, 'Let this mind be in you which was also in Christ Jesus' (Phil 2:5), and he now realised beyond any doubt that that was what he wanted for himself. He enthusiastically embraced this new way of life, trusting the words of St Paul, 'He whose power is at work in us is powerful enough, and more than powerful enough, to carry out his purpose, beyond all our hopes and dreams' (Eph 3:20).

Soon after entering the novitiate John, along with the other new novices, made the Spiritual Exercises of St Ignatius, frequently known as the Long Retreat. Lasting for thirty days, it was probably the most profound experience of his novitiate, if not his life. John had spent many years searching for God's will, and now he was eager to learn more about the way in which God was leading him and to follow it. During the retreat John spent many hours contemplating the life of Christ, becoming keenly aware of the Lord's goodness and mercy, how he touched people with his life-giving love, how in poverty and personal suffering he gave his life for others and how he rose again to new life. John prayed to be called to share in Christ's mission, if that was God's will, and to offer himself wholeheartedly for service.

Influence of the Novice Master

The novice master's role in the Long Retreat retreat, as practised at that time, was to propose the matter for prayer, but without imposing in any way on the novice. Fr Michael Browne, John's novice master, was only a little older than himself, and they resembled each other in many ways. He was to be a model and inspiration for his novice. John learned from him to pay little regard to his ordinary human needs and weaknesses, and to offer himself as a gift to God – and for God to his fellow men and women.

Fr Browne was an ascetical figure who practised self-denial and mortification to a heroic degree. He rose early in the morning, but ate nothing before ten o'clock, and then only a few dry crusts. Later in the day, he would allow himself only one meal. In his own life, John was similarly ascetical, mostly eating only dry bread, milk puddings and porridge; he drank only cold water. He allowed no relaxation on Sundays or feast days. He ate no meat or anything sweet, and never enjoyed any variety. His boots were many times repaired, and his clothes were old and shabby, but always immaculately clean and well darned. It is thought that John never asked for new clothes during the whole of his life as a Jesuit.

This austerity, modelled on the example of his novice master, was John's way of emptying himself in order to be filled with Christ. In Fr Browne, John had found an advisor who taught him how to combat temptation and to keep his focus on imitating Christ. His debt to Fr Browne was immense, as he later revealed on one of the very few occasions when he spoke about himself. 'Without him,' he admitted, 'I'd never have stuck it out.'

Scholastic Years
On 8 September 1902, John pronounced his first vows and moved immediately to Stonyhurst, in England, to study philosophy. Because of his age and his previous years of study – he was a very late vocation in those days – his formation course was abbreviated to seven years instead of the usual sixteen or so. From the start, his instinctive generosity was noted in his new community. He wanted to serve others whenever possible, undertaking a duty on their behalf, anticipating a need, or offering assistance. His new companions apparently did not always appreciate these overtures, suspecting that

they implied criticism of their own willingness or ability to perform the tasks involved. They soon learned otherwise, however, recognising John's charitable intentions and coming to look on him with affection. They were deeply impressed by his commitment to prayer. One young Jesuit spoke of how he came unobserved into the chapel one day and watched John at prayer, his eyes fixed on the tabernacle and his lips moving silently. Another companion remarked that 'one felt that here was a man that lived and walked with God'.

Soon John was on his way back to Dublin, to Milltown Park, where he studied theology. He was now only three years away from ordination. It was eleven years since he had been received into the Catholic Church, and twenty-eight years since his graduation from Portora, where he had first intuited a call from God. We might be tempted to think that it took a needlessly long time for him to reach this point, but John's ordination card suggests otherwise. Taken from Psalm 116, it reads, 'What shall I render to the Lord for all the things he hath rendered to me?' His choice of this passage is surely significant. The new priest is not concerned about the long years he has spent searching for God, but rejoices instead in all that God has done for him. Not only that, he is also looking ahead to envision what he might now be able to do for God in return. He has come a long way. Learning to have 'that mind that was also in Christ Jesus' takes time, and the self-emptying that is required involves long, and sometimes painful, learning. John is now ready to move to a new phase of his life.

First Years in Clongowes

One might imagine that for John, who was a gold medallist in both Portora and Trinity, teaching Latin and Greek would be a labour of love. In fact the next twelve years, which he spent in Clongowes Wood College, a boarding school situated in a remote area, found him struggling among uncomprehending schoolboys. Adolescent boys rarely find Latin grammar or Greek syntax interesting, and John was unwilling to be the tough disciplinarian that one of his colleagues advised.

John probably never understood boys of that age anyway, and he was not considered to be an effective teacher. He was an outsider to their lives, did not understand their humour and did not have the gift for the happy phrase. He had no real interest in what someone called 'the small change' of school life – the daily events of the classroom and the playing field that can dominate schoolboy conversation. John did not watch their games, nor did he attend their debates or concerts, or watch their plays. In class, his students found ways of distracting him from what he was teaching, and they had some fun by playing tricks on him, occasionally causing chaos. One of the 'little devils' involved later wondered, 'Were we sorry? I think we were a little ashamed at heart, but it didn't show in that early adolescent stage of the struggle to avoid education'.

If John was not successful in the classroom, it was an inspired choice to appoint him Spiritual Father to the students in Clongowes in 1909. His task now was to look after the spiritual welfare of the boys and to take an interest in their personal development. This new role suited him perfectly, and his impact was immense. 'Veneration' is the only appropriate word to express the sentiments of generations of Clongownians towards him from then on.

John's kindness was legendary, and the boys quickly learned that he would do anything for them. Matthias Bodkin, who knew him both as a boy and later as a young Jesuit in Rathfarnham, remarked that 'once a boy turned to him for help he could feel complete confidence of his reception ... When a homesick new boy was out of sorts or worried about some mishap, Fr Sullivan's room was the place where he could forget his troubles ... (John) seemed to understand disappointments, upsets, homesickness or mere loneliness'. The boys may have been amused by his outward demeanour and the strange way he walked – shuffling along at speed, as if to waste no time – but of one thing they were sure: he was a saint.

Rector of Rathfarnham Castle
In 1919, John was moved to Rathfarnham Castle in Dublin where, much to his surprise, he was appointed rector of a large community of young Jesuits who were attending university. John's example impressed

the young men from the start. They were aware of his meagre diet of dried bread, porridge, potatoes and rice. They knew that he had no heating in his draughty room even in the depths of winter. They saw him as a saint, one who peered somewhat uneasily at the world of the senses and seemed to have trouble bringing his mind to bear on anything other than spiritual realities. They would always be grateful for the precious experience of knowing John Sullivan.

As well as his duties as rector, John busied himself giving talks and directing retreats, mainly to other religious. While giving these talks, he kept his gaze fixed, not on his audience, but on the crucifix he grasped in his hands. This crucifix, which had been given to him by his mother, was also the crucifix he received with his vows. While in Rathfarnham, John also got involved with St Mary's open-air hospital for children, and he came to be a firm supporter of Frank Duff and the Legion of Mary. Perhaps surprisingly, he also had a retreat house built for working men in Rathfarnham Castle, fulfilling the dream of another Jesuit, Fr Willie Doyle, who had been killed while serving as chaplain in the First World War.

Return to Clongowes
Responsibility for a large community probably weighed heavily on John's shoulders, and it is likely that it was with relief that he was sent back to Clongowes, in 1924, again as Spiritual Father to the boys. Shortly afterwards, he was given an additional responsibility, which proved to be providential. He was put in charge of the People's Church, a small church attached to the school that served the local people. It was this appointment that would bring him into close contact with the local community and the wider population, giving him the chance to express his love of God through the service of those who were suffering or in need. It is this part of his life that has left the most vivid impression, not only on local people, but on many others throughout Ireland and further afield.

From the start, John made himself available without question to anyone who came for his assistance. Word spread quickly among the local people that they had among them a holy priest to whom they could come with whatever troubles they had, whether of mind or body. They knew where to find him too, for he spent long hours in the confessional, or on his knees before the altar, or giving a blessing at the holy water font. They came in great numbers: some on tottering feet, some by harnessed horse or ass, some by bicycle, a few in motor cars.

He didn't just wait for them to come to him, however; he went out to them as well. According to Fr Bodkin, John would answer without hesitation any cry of distress that came to him, sometimes cycling long distances to comfort a person in need. He would frequently return to a sick or dying person, day after day, if the pain was great or the dying prolonged. He sometimes brought small gifts of tea, sugar or clothing to those who were struggling to survive in a time of great poverty. As he arrived at the house, shuffling along in his usual fashion, he would greet the family briefly and then head for the sick-room. Always he would bless the room with lots of holy water, and then he would spend some time – often an hour or longer – in silent prayer. After confession, if the sick person asked for it, the family would gather around to recite the rosary or to say prayers of trust and thanksgiving. John would then slip away quietly, never drawing attention to himself.

The people came to believe that this holy priest, who was so patently close to God, not only healed souls, but had the gift of healing bodies as well. Stories of cures that were worked through his mediation are legion, and were subsequently passed on from generation to generation with unwavering conviction. One such story tells of a telegram arriving to John in Clongowes at eleven o'clock one morning. It informed him of a young sister novice who had been involved in a most serious accident and was in danger of death. John left by bike immediately, and by early afternoon had arrived at the hospital in Dublin, some thirty kilometres away. He went straight to the young sister's room, fell on his knees and began to pray. Some hours later, it was noted that the patient's condition had begun to change. First, the delirium ceased, then the restless tossing and turning ended, and finally a peaceful sleep came over her. Now that she was out of danger, John slipped away, without pausing for any nourishment, reaching Clongowes that evening in time for a meeting of the Sodality of our Lady.

Account after account of John's visits repeat the salient features of that story: the dramatic appeal for his help, the spontaneous response, the long prayerful vigil, the recovery of the patient, and finally the rapid departure without accepting any refreshment. It was not that John was ungrateful, but he had to be about his Father's business and he knew that others might be waiting for him.

And frequently there were others waiting for him, as demands for his presence and prayers increased. Innumerable stories testify to the unshakable faith people had in this humble man who, they believed, was an instrument of peace in God's hands, and of bodily healing too.

After his Death

People's faith in John's healing gifts did not diminish after his death in 1933. From the start, many began to come to visit his grave, which was situated near the main entrance to Clongowes. Often they left a memento – a rosary, a scapular or a medal – behind them as a prayerful gesture. Others took a small amount of clay from the grave itself to bring to a suffering relative. From far and near they came to pray and to ask his intercession for themselves or their loved ones, just as they had done when he was alive.

The cause for the beatification of Fr John Sullivan was introduced in 1944, and his remains were transferred to St Francis Xavier Church in Gardiner Street, Dublin, in 1960. There, devotion to him continued as before, with people coming to pray at his tomb and often requesting a blessing with the cross he had frequently clasped in his hands. The demand for a blessing with this cross has continued unabated ever since.

Among the many reported cures attributed to the intercession of John Sullivan, one was thoroughly documented and investigated by Church authorities, and was eventually declared to be genuine. This opened the way to the day that many had hoped for: in 2016 he was declared Blessed John Sullivan.

PART FOUR

North America

~ 8 ~

A Failure Redeemed:
Jean de Brébeuf SJ (1593–1649)

David Stewart SJ

Throughout the sixteenth century, and until the suppression of the Society of Jesus in 1773, Jesuit missionary activity was daring, creative and enterprising. From the Society's beginning in 1540, mobility and flexibility were to be its characteristics. Jesuits were typically on the move – or ready to move – 'to the ends of the earth'. Jerome Nadal, one of the earliest and most insightful interpreters of Ignatius, once noted that the Jesuit's true home is not a fixed abode but rather the highway. More recently, a Jesuit has been characterised as 'one who is sent, called and missioned, and ideally ready to go anywhere'.

A Larger World Revealed

The founder of the Jesuits, Ignatius Loyola, was born just as Europe was about to discover that it was only a small part of a much greater world. He was born – 1491 is the generally accepted date – at the time when Columbus was about to head westward on his momentous voyage of discovery. During the following century, astonishing reports frequently reached the great cities and centres of learning in Europe, describing new lands and unknown people, their unfamiliar customs and different cultures. They were exciting times.

As the extent of the greater world gradually revealed itself to Europeans, the Jesuits' highway was seen to be much longer and more unpredictable than previously envisaged. They were far from being starry-eyed about what lay before them, however. They prepared themselves over many years, for the what lay ahead, using the spiritual insights that Ignatius had bequeathed to them, especially through his Spiritual Exercises. They were challenged to shake off their self-centred attachments and free themselves from 'disordered affections', in Ignatius's words. Instead, they were to embrace true freedom, the freedom to serve as Jesus served. That freedom was ordered towards the mission.

It must have been an intriguing time for Jean de Brébeuf, who was born into a comfortable farming family in Normandy in 1593. During his boyhood and years of schooling, he must have heard many stories about the strange lands that had been discovered, becoming fascinated by the different peoples that lay beyond the shores of his native France. The world, he must have realised, was much bigger and more diverse – and not simply geographically – than the self-contained Europe people had known in earlier generations.

Early Years as a Jesuit

Brébeuf's Jesuit life began after his university studies, at the comparatively late age of twenty-four. He remained in Normandy, in northwestern France, for the early phases of his Jesuit formation, beginning with the novitiate in Rouen in 1617. It appears that he thought seriously about becoming a brother rather than a priest, seeing it as a humbler way to serve the Lord and possibly more suited to his gifts. His superiors thought otherwise, however, and insisted that he become a scholastic, destined for the priesthood.

Novices are typically fired up by dreams of what they might do for Christ – it's a theme that runs right through the Spiritual Exercises – and Jean was certainly no different. Those dreams were foundational for his vocation, but he still had to refine them and make them concrete in his life, as the Jesuit *Constitutions* encouraged. That would be one of the tasks of his years of formation.

During those years, he was surely inspired by the stories he heard about the exploits of the previous generations of Jesuits and, in particular, by the story of that greatest of all Jesuit missionaries, St Francis Xavier. Ignatius encouraged Jesuits to write frequently to each other, and not just to the superior general in Rome. The purpose of this was to disseminate information, to inspire enthusiasm and to build up the apostolic body – a custom that, mutatis mutandis, continues to this day. It was because of these letters that the story of Francis Xavier became widely known at that time. Xavier was an inspiring figure. At short notice, he had set off for the Far East as a substitute for another Jesuit who had suddenly fallen ill. It must have been thrilling for Brébeuf and his fellow scholastics to hear of Xavier's reaction when Ignatius chose him for this daunting mission: 'I'm ready – send me'.

Arrival in Canada

It was in that spirit that Brébeuf set off, in the spring of 1625, together with several other Jesuits, on his two-month voyage to Québec. The Jesuits had first reached the region known as New France in 1611, but the first order to reach Québec itself were the Franciscan Recollects, who had arrived there in 1615. Indeed, it was in response to an appeal from the Recollects that Brébeuf and his companions set off on their long and treacherous journey across the Atlantic. Having arrived in Québec, they then continued onwards for more than 1,000 kilometres towards the Huron territory.

Brébeuf's dream was to evangelise the Hurons, a powerful nation that had strong trading links with the French colonists in New France. The Hurons were accustomed to paying an annual visit to the French settlements, where they would barter furs and other goods in exchange for European products, and Brébeuf decided that this would be the ideal opportunity for him to make significant contact with them. Until that opportunity arrived, Brébeuf set about befriending another tribe, the Montaignais people. He accompanied them on their hunting expeditions, came to understand their ways and learned their language – something that came easily to him, for he was known to have a talent for languages. All this time, he was beginning to adapt himself to this land – so different from flat, pastoral Normandy – and its cruel winter climate.

Establishing the Huron Mission

Brébeuf was a large man. Fearful that their canoe might be capsized on account of his bulk, the Hurons were initially reluctant to take him with them as they set out on their return journey from Québec. Eventually, persuaded by his pleading and by the many gifts he brought, they agreed to allow him to join them insisting, however, that he sit perfectly still in the canoe. Several times as they negotiated the rivers they encountered waterfalls, which involved carrying all their goods overland until they reached calmer waters again. On these occasions, their passenger astounded them by the huge loads he could carry. Almost inevitably, he attracted the Huron nickname '*Echon*', which means, 'the man who carries large loads'. Ironically, his physical appearance would later contribute to the manner of his martyrdom.

On reaching Huronia, Brébeuf once again employed his language skills. As he pondered how best to evangelise the people, he resolved to spend two whole years studying their language, customs and beliefs. Before long he was teaching the Huron language to other missionaries, and he later compiled a grammar of the Huron Language and translated a catechism into that language as well. Everything seemed to be in place for a successful mission, but all was not as it appeared.

The Jesuit approach to evangelisation was to enter deeply into the culture of the people and understand their customs and beliefs. This approach, while praiseworthy, frequently proved to be a risky one. Brébeuf hoped to transmit the Christian Gospel through the culture and language of the people, but he found that progress was disappointingly slow. While many of the Hurons welcomed his interest in them, others resisted his involvement, and some resented his presence altogether, seeing him as a threat to their own leadership positions. Another obstacle arose because of the diseases that had recently arrived from Europe, and from which the Hurons had no immunity. These had begun to spread throughout the community, adding to the growing suspicion that the 'Blackrobes', as the Jesuits were called, were responsible. Only a handful of people – mostly those who were sick or dying – accepted baptism, and this gave his opponents the opportunity to distort the message further, presenting it as another form of sorcery.

Unexpected Return to France

At this stage, international politics intervened, as so often happened in these missionary endeavours. War had broken out between England and France, and in the summer of 1629 English ships had blockaded the St Lawrence River, limiting food supplies and threatening famine in the region. Hearing this news, Brébeuf set sail for Québec with a number of canoes laden with Huron wheat. The well-intentioned relief effort proved fruitless, however, for as soon as he arrived at his destination he learned that the French had capitulated to the English forces. As a result, all French settlers and missionaries were to be repatriated to France, and Brébeuf found himself, in 1629, unexpectedly on a ship back to France.

It is not known how Brébeuf reacted to this threat to his dream for the mission in New France, but he may well have taken inspiration from a story he had surely heard about the founder of his order. Ignatius had once famously declared that, were the fledgling Society of Jesus to be suppressed, he thought that fifteen minutes of prayer before the Blessed Sacrament would be enough for him to accept such a setback with equilibrium. That story may have helped Brébeuf as he struggled with his own disappointment. In the event, shortly after his return to France, he was sent to teach in a Jesuit school in Rouen where, undoubtedly, he astounded his young charges with fantastic tales of those northern lands across the ocean. He also longed for an opportunity to return some day.

The Return to the Mission

That opportunity came a few years later following the Treaty of Saint-Germain-en-Laye, signed in 1632. This treaty restored Québec and the other territories captured by the English to French control, opening the way for renewed missionary activity. Despite these developments, Brébeuf had to wait almost a further year before he could return to North America. When he did, he was entrusted by his superior, Fr Paul Le Jeune, with the establishment of a fixed mission centre in the Huron country. For this, Brébeuf chose a site in Ihonatiria, near Toanché in present-day Ontario, close to the shore of Lake Huron. He called the mission after St Joseph.

Once again, nothing went smoothly for him. Several epidemics of influenza, smallpox and dysentery had broken out in the region, resulting in as many as 18,000 deaths, according to the Jesuits' estimates. Some of the Hurons began a campaign of violent threats against the Jesuits, arguing that these disasters were the fault of the missionaries.

As time went on, threats against the Jesuits grew. The view developed that these 'Blackrobes' were malevolent sorcerers. It was put about that they had deliberately caused the epidemic to deplete Huron numbers and thus to subjugate them more easily. Things worsened for the missionaries as further epidemics afflicted the Hurons, particularly a major smallpox outbreak in 1639. The Jesuits' churches were attacked and burnt.There is on record a letter from Brébeuf to Fr Le Jeune, in which he predicts the massacre of all the Jesuits.

Local Hostilities

As well as the outbreak of major epidemics, another factor, political in nature, entered the picture. The Hurons, trading partners and close allies of the French, had long been at war with another powerful nation, the Iroquois. To protect their trade, the French were committed to lending military support to the Hurons and, by extension, to their war against the Iroquois. Although they had no role in this bitter dispute, the Jesuits became unintentionally embroiled in it. At one stage, Brébeuf was accused of colluding with the Iroquois and betraying the Hurons. By the mid-1640s, Huron chiefs were agitating for the removal, by whatever means, of the Jesuits from their territories, believing that all their misfortunes could be traced to their presence.

Security was collapsing fast as suspicion and violence was spreading. The martyrdom of two Jesuits, Br René Goupil and Fr Isaac Jogues, would follow in 1642 and 1646 respectively. In view of the fraught situation, it was judged best that Brébeuf be evacuated back to Québec for a time until the atmosphere improved. While there he organised supplies for the Jesuits who remained in the mission station, waiting all the time for an opportunity to return. In fact, the situation in the mission territories continued to be highly volatile.

In a further attempt to evangelise the Hurons, Brébeuf returned for a final time to their territory in May 1644. On that occasion he was accompanied by Fr Antoine Daniel, who would be martyred in July 1648. Serious problems remained, however. The Christian symbols and the actions of the missionaries were misunderstood by some people, while the missionaries themselves did not always know how to interpret the Hurons' local customs. On one occasion, as we shall see, the advent of rain, following a novena of prayers to alleviate a severe drought, was interpreted in ways the missionaries had not anticipated. Fr Paul Ragueneau, the third superior of the mission, noted the underlying problem faced by so many missionaries at that time. 'One must be very careful,' he wrote, 'before condemning a thousand things among their customs, which greatly offend minds nurtured and set in another world … I have no hesitation in saying that we have been too severe on this point.'

A Horrific Martyrdom

By the middle of the decade the Iroquois, supported by arms supplied by Dutch traders who were in competition with their French counterparts, had succeeded in asserting their superiority in the region. This resulted in ever more instability. In March 1649, Brébeuf was ministering at the outstation of Saint-Louis when news came of an attack by 1,000 Iroquois on another outstation, Saint-Ignace. With him on that occasion was a recently arrived Jesuit, Gabriel Lalemant, who himself would be face martyrdom the day after Brébeuf's death. Shortly afterwards, at a time when most of the Huron warriors were away, the Iroquois invaded Saint-Ignace. Local leaders urged the Jesuits to hide in the forest with the women and children, but they insisted on remaining behind.

The two Jesuits were captured. A renegade Huron, who had gone over to the enemy forces, had spread it abroad that this giant of a man, Echon, was the most powerful sorcerer that the Hurons had, one who could even end a drought when their own people had been powerless. According to the spy, this meant that Brébeuf deserved the most vicious death possible, involving prolonged torture before the end came. The *Dictionary of Canadian Biography* preserves this account from another witness, one Christophe Regnault, a lay volunteer.

> Father de Brébeuf had his legs, thighs, and arms stripped of flesh to the very bone; I saw and touched a large number of great blisters, which he had on several places on his body, from the boiling water which these barbarians had poured over him in mockery of Holy Baptism. I saw and touched the wound from a belt of bark, full of pitch and resin, which roasted his whole body. I saw and touched the marks of burns from the collar of hatchets placed on his shoulders and stomach. I saw and touched his two lips, which they had cut off because he constantly spoke of God while they made him suffer. I saw and touched all parts of his body, which had received more than two hundred blows from a stick. I saw and touched the top of his scalped head; I saw and touched the opening which these barbarians had made to tear out his heart.

An End or a Beginning?

The Huron nation fell to pieces after these attacks, dispersed and humiliated after further epidemics, famines and fresh asaults. The remaining missionaries left for Québec, their mission ended. Fr Jean de Brébeuf's remains were removed to Québec in 1650. It seemed that all the Jesuits' efforts had been in vain.

And yet it wasn't so. By some strange working of providence, in the following decades the dispersed Hurons played a significant part in bringing the gospel message to the nations of the Great Lakes area including, ironically, the Iroquois themselves. The numbers of those being baptised, which had been disappointing during Brébeuf's lifetime, began to increase massively, with as many as 3,000 baptisms recorded in one year alone. The mission, it seemed, had taken on a new and unexpected life after all had seemed lost. The blood of Jean de Brébeuf and his fellow Jesuit martyrs, the first saints of North America, truly was the seed of the faith in that continent.

In 1930, Pope Pius XII canonised Jean de Brébeuf, along with seven other Jesuits martyred in New France between 1642 and 1649. He is now venerated as one of the patron saints of Canada.

~ 9 ~
Engaging with Modernity:
Bernard Lonergan SJ (1904–1984)

Gerry O'Hanlon SJ

Like his contemporary Karl Rahner, Bernard Lonergan lived most of his life in the early part of the twentieth century, before the Second Vatican Council took place. Those years formed part of what historian John O'Malley has called the 'long nineteenth century' of the Catholic Church. It was a time when the official Church viewed modernity with suspicion, and lived out of a largely defensive, self-sufficient stance that was resolutely opposed to the perceived errors of the surrounding culture. Lonergan was one of those Catholic intellectuals who succeeded in bringing this mostly self-enclosed culture into dialogue with the modern world, without sacrificing its distinctive identity. He did so largely by focusing, in both philosophy and theology, on questions of foundations and method.

Earlier Years

Bernard Lonergan's great-grandparents, Timothy Lonergan and Bridget Casey, were both Irish immigrants who settled in Ste-Thérèse-de-Blainville, a town near Montreal, early in the nineteenth century. His parents, Gerald and Josephine, were married in

Buckingham, situated 150 kilometres east of Montreal, when Bernard, their first child, was born in 1904. After a schooling that evidenced his abilities in mathematics and science in particular, he entered the Jesuit novitiate in Guelph, Ontario, in 1922. As part of his Jesuit formation he studied philosophy in Heythrop College, Oxfordshire, from 1926 to 1929. It was during those years that he developed a desire to understand the problem of knowledge, a problem that had been raised in particular by the empiricists, who emphasised the role of sensory experience in knowing, and also by the Kant's 'Copernican revolution', which stressed the subjective nature of human knowing.

In different ways, these two strands of philosophy had come to dominate the secular academic scene and had, increasingly, influenced the culture as a whole. As he explored the subject, Lonergan began to understand that the propositional, logical approach of Neo-Thomism, then normative within Catholic seminaries, did not address their positions adequately. It was around this time, and seemingly by chance, that he came across Newman's *Grammar of Assent*, and began to grasp that Newman's 'illative sense' – the human capacity to judge – offered a way forward in researching the fundamental problem of knowledge. It was from these beginnings that his theory of 'critical realism' emerged, resulting in his major philosophical work *Insight: A Study of Human Understanding*, begun formally in 1949.

Broad Intellectual Interests
Lonergan did his undergraduate and postgraduate theological studies in Rome in the 1930s, and it became clear by 1938, in view of his outstanding gifts, that his mission as a Jesuit would be in the intellectual apostolate. During this period – influenced by the economic depression in the United States, and later by the outbreak of war and the rise of totalitarian states – he renewed what would be a lifelong interest in economics and political economy. This interest fed into another interest of his, the philosophy of history, and this in turn, through his encounter with the thought of Aquinas on

operative grace, opened the way to theological considerations and to elucidating the link between theology and philosophy.

In 1940, Lonergan began a career of teaching and writing that would last for forty-three years. He started first in Montreal, then at the Gregorian University in Rome, and finally back on the North American continent, mainly in Boston and Toronto. The first draft of *Insight* was completed in 1953, but publication was delayed until March 1957.

In the meantime, Lonergan had shifted gear. In 1953, he was sent back to Rome to teach theology, and he began more and more to focus on that discipline rather than philosophy. More specifically, after some years teaching courses on the Trinity and the Incarnation, he began to see that there were links between his positions on philosophical foundations, the notion of history, and theological method.

Personal Crises

The crisis year of 1965, when he had a dramatic and life-threatening encounter with lung cancer, was particularly important for Lonergan. Following three major operations in Toronto, he was eventually restored to good health and his intellectual pursuits, although not in Rome. It was during this crisis that he received major insights into what theological method is about, assisted not least by what he came to consider the providential, deeply loving care of a nursing sister, Sr Florian, at the hospital in Toronto.

While Longeran had many friends, male and female, it seems that during this critical time he had a profound experience of being truly cared for, a sense of being loved by another person that was quite outside his normal intellectual horizons and experiences. This experience considerably influenced his later repeated assertion that religion was primarily the experience of the love of God and that faith is the knowledge born of religious love.

Less happily, his excruciating experience of suffering led him for a while to an increasing dependence on alcohol. After the successful publication of his major theological work in 1973, *Method in Theology*, he asked to receive treatment for this addiction.

Critical Realism

In terms of Lonergan's intellectual achievements, there was, first of all, his challenge to the approaches dominant in the secular world of modernity, which Neo-Scholasticism was ill-equipped to combat. He identified two such trends in particular. On the one hand, there was empiricism, or 'naïve realism', which limited its contents to the material world, and considered knowing to be 'taking a look' at the 'already-out-there-now-real'. On the other hand, there was the post-Kantian approach – idealism – that, in its 'turn to the subject', risked sacrificing the objectivity of human knowledge. In this view, the intelligible order we seem to find in the world is largely attributed to the activity of the human mind; intelligibility is there only as the imposition of a conceptual framework. Lonergan took issue with both of these positions, and suggested an alternative approach. By means of a process of self-appropriation, he invited readers to identify in themselves and others the invariant cognitional pattern or structure present in every human subject, across every field of knowledge, allowing them to know the real objective world.

Often using examples from science and mathematics, but also from other fields of life, Lonergan identifies in *Insight* the crucial cognitional structure common to us all. We begin with experience, Lonergan points out; then we ask questions about that experience, leading to a hypothesis; we then reflect on our hunch, and go on to make a judgement about its truth; finally, we ask what we are to do about the truth we have affirmed, what is the right path to choose. In Lonergan's analysis, then, the universal cognitional structure involves experience and attention to data in the first place, then insight and understanding of the same, followed by judgement about whether all the relevant questions have been asked and if the understanding can be affirmed as true, leading finally to a decision about how to proceed responsibly in light of the affirmed truth. This process he sums up in his 'four transcendental imperatives': be attentive, be intelligent, be reasonable, be responsible.

Lonergan argues that the different operations of this four-fold structure are all conscious, since they involve an awareness of the subject as experiencing, understanding, judging and deciding. They do not stop at ideas or concepts only, however, for they are united in their intentionality towards being or the real. He argues that an intellectual conversion is involved in coming to this insight into human knowledge, with its emphasis on the crucial role of judgement. He notes that the four transcendental precepts are activities of the human subject – not, as in Neo-Scholasticism, logical first principles of a conceptual nature – and that they are the conditions of being an authentic person capable of making objective judgements about the real world. 'Genuine objectivity', he writes, 'is the fruit of authentic subjectivity.'

Over years of study and reflection, and influenced by St Thomas, Newman and Maréchal, Lonergan developed these thoughts and produced his enormous and closely argued volume, *Insight*, in the mid-1950s. This gave many thinkers from the Catholic tradition, and from other Christian traditions as well, the confidence to dialogue with the world of modernity and to challenge its reduction of knowledge and the real to what is material only. Furthermore – and already prescient of what post-modernity would offer – it enabled these thinkers to honour the 'anthropological turn', common since Descartes and Kant, while avoiding the kind of relativism common to this approach, which too often resulted in a limitation of knowledge to subjective viewpoints only.

History: Progress and Decline

Lonergan was well aware – not least through the ups and downs of his own life and times – that human authenticity and self-transcendence were not simply a matter of intellectual conversion. In contrast to the myth of universal progress, common in modernity, he understood history in terms of progress and decline. He noted in particular the perennial blocks to freedom and understanding that are characteristic of history.

These blocks or 'biases' can occur at different levels, and they shape the dialectics of individual and social history. He notes three such biases in particular: 'individual bias', which means putting oneself at the centre of the universe and acting accordingly; 'group bias', a distorted way of addressing the world by adopting the exclusive perspective of one's own group, culture or locality; and general or 'common-sense bias', a preference for short-term pragmatism at the expense of ever getting to the root of things.

In considering social and economic history, Lonergan offers a sombre reading of the modern world as urgently in need of faith and redemption. He notes that the outcome of bias is a cumulative but unconscious compromise, both on the individual and the cultural levels. If unrecognised, it produces impotence and ideology, and can even 'menace civilization with destruction'. Where a communal flight from understanding happens, he argues, stagnation takes over and situations head towards crisis and even war. So, while human self-transcendence offers a dynamic towards progress, bias tends to limit or even destroy the freedom to imagine life differently. Ultimately, Lonergan argues, this freedom is dependent on the reality that God has entered into the chaos of human history. The mystery of existence and the problem of evil only find resolution in the existence of God.

Lonergan's attention to history and its tensions – which he calls, possibly in dialogue with Hegel, 'dialectics' – involves a move away from a classicism which prizes uniformity, homogeneity and normative sameness, towards a respect for what is distinctive and singular, and ultimately for what is culturally pluralistic. With his process-based cognitional theory and his respect for the movement of history, Lonergan's approach opened paths to developments in many different fields, including interdisciplinary and doctrinal studies.

It is interesting to note that, although they were not connected on any explicit level, a similar dynamic was going on in the pre-Vatican Council proponents of the 'nouvelle théologie'. This group – among them theologians like Henri de Lubac and Yves Congar, who were highly influential at the Second Vatican Council – refused to be bound exclusively by the normative, 'classical' approach to theology, with its focus on Aquinas through the lens of Neo-Scholasticism. Rather, through the process that came to be known as *ressourcement*

– a return to the sources – they were nourished by a retrieval of patristic, scriptural and liturgical sources. This attention to a wider history made it possible to imagine a different future for the Church, and a less rigid definition of tradition, at the council.

Method in Theology

For many years Lonergan taught theology according to the given neo-scholastic way of establishing a system of propositions from Scripture, patristic writings, Church teaching and the consensus of theologians. As modernity shaded into post-modernity, however, he was uneasy with the results, and saw the need to engage with historical scholarship (including biblical criticism and the history of doctrines), hermeneutics and, above all, religious experience. Students, he began to see, were simply bored by a propositional theology which wasn't 'religious', and which left to one side the involvement of the person. This development in Lonergan's thinking was taking place around the time when the Decree on Revelation of the Second Vatican Council was being formulated. That decree spoke of divine revelation more in terms of an encounter with the mystery and person of Jesus Christ than a set of unchanging propositions held in the 'deposit of faith'.

It was about that time too that Lonergan was struck by a remark of one of his students. Acknowledging that he was beginning to understand the crucial distinction between questions for understanding and those for judgement in cognitional theory, this student went on to point out that 'when a man is in love, he is always asking *"who* are you?"' And so, gradually, the passionate intellectualism of *Insight* began, not least through his own experience of illness and love in 1965, to develop into *Method in Theology*, published in 1973. Here there is a new emphasis on feelings and love. 'Intermediate between judgements of fact and judgements of value lie apprehensions of value,' wrote Lonergan. 'Such apprehensions are given in feelings'.

In terms of his understanding of the 'differentiation of consciousness', Lonergan was now moving between the realms of theory and interiority. The theologian is a member of a religious community and culture, and of a human community that at every point in its history is faced with the challenge of differentiating between progress and decline. In this context theology becomes a reflection on the religion of a culture, a reflection on religious experience.

This religious experience varies from culture to culture, class to class, person to person. Rooted in God's gift of love, it is antecedent to any knowledge of God, for 'religious experience, at its root, is an experience of an unconditioned and unrestricted being in love'. If intellectual and even moral conversion are experienced more as an *upward* movement of striving and achievement, religious conversion is experienced more as a *downward* movement, whereby we receive a gift, a gift that transforms everything. Faith, in that context, is 'the knowledge born of religious love'. The transforming experience of religious love enables a self-transcendence to take place, corresponding to the 'eros of the human spirit', bringing about a shift from a life of purposeless drifting to a life of commitment to values – a life of true authenticity.

Lonergan proceeds to develop in *Method* a notion of theology as mediating between culture and religious experience, with what he calls eight 'functional specialities'. These specialities – research, interpretation, history, dialectic, foundations, doctrines, systematics and communications – correspond to the four levels of human conscious operations as already outlined in *Insight*, but with a new emphasis on the fourth level of moral consciousness, the understanding of which is enhanced by the new emphasis on religious conversion and love. This experience of religious conversion is reflected on most explicitly in his treatment of 'foundations'.

Unlike *Insight*, *Method in Theology* is somewhat programmatic and minimalist in its approach, and it is left to others to develop its potentiality.

A Powerful Legacy

It is clear that Lonergan himself understood his intellectual life as central to his Christian and Jesuit vocation, and he was supported in this by his religious superiors. It is also clear that the fruits of his labours were immensely beneficial. The publication of *Insight* was a major event in twentieth century Catholic scholarship. It enabled Catholic philosophers and theologians to engage with modernity, in particular with the restrictive limitations which empiricism and idealism imposed on the human capacity to know the real world and to search for ultimate meaning.

Then, as Post-Modernism arrived and the council's effects began to be felt, Lonergan's *Method* opened up new possibilities for an engagement between theology and the surrounding culture, not least by positing an unchanging, universal way of proceeding – 'method' – which yet respected the pluralism and specificity of different cultures. Post-Modernism can easily disintegrate into cultural fragmentation, with little awareness of the viewpoints of others or of the wider common good. Lonergan's focus on religious experience, and on the invariant patterns of human knowing and loving, offers a way to honour Post-Modernism's respect for diversity and the individual, without conceding to its despair about objectivity and the good of society. It may be said, then, that it was the peculiar genius of Lonergan, both in his philosophical and theological writings, to lay foundations which, in principle, enable others to construct transcendental approaches to meaning which would be respectful of contemporary realities and also faithful to the dynamics of biblical revelation.

Lonergan remains one of the largely unknown giants of twentieth century theology. His work on foundations was never likely to reach a wide public and, while he has had enormous influence within certain Christian circles, he is largely unknown in the secular world. It remains to be seen whether that will change. The increasing recognition of the creative moment of insight in scientific enquiry, the post-modern focus on experience as primary, and the requirement for a cross-cultural theology are all points upon which Lonergan has much to offer.

Most of all, perhaps, Lonergan has something significant to offer us today in Ireland, and in many other traditionally Christian cultures. His espousal of a critical realism that respects subjectivity but not at the expense of objective truth, his respect for history, and his ability to do theology in dialogue with culture, these offer hope that the gospel revelation can still be communicated as good news to the nations. This is what Paul did at the Areopagus in ancient Athens (Acts 17:23–31); it's what generations of Christians have tried to do ever since; and it's what we are all called to do in our own time, unless we resign ourselves to becoming, in Archbishop Diarmuid Martin's eloquent words, 'an irrelevant cultural minority'.

~ 10 ~
An Open-Ended Thinker:
John Courtney Murray SJ (1904–1967)

Gerard Whelan SJ

In 2013, a remarkable event occurred: a Jesuit was elected pope. In his role as pope, Francis is called to lead the universal Church, but to do this he draws deeply on his Jesuit identity. Early in his pontificate he gave a wide-ranging interview to a Jesuit journalist, Antonio Spadaro, in which he explained how deeply his pastoral vision is rooted in the Spiritual Exercises of St Ignatius. In particular, he spoke of the importance of the Ignatian practice of discernment of spirits for his way of proceeding. Elaborating on this conviction, he spoke of the importance for Jesuits, at an intellectual level, of engaging in 'open-ended thinking'. He explained that this involves recognising that one's life is always in process, so that one rarely knows in advance the problems to be faced, much less what the answers to these problems will be.

Pope Francis then makes a more general point: 'God manifests himself in time and is present in the processes of history. This gives priority to actions that give birth to new historical dynamics. And it requires patience, waiting.' He then contrasts this approach to 'closed and rigid thinking'. Subsequently, in his apostolic exhortation *Evangelii Gaudium*, Pope Francis draws again on many of these ideas, and suggests that it is important that all pastoral agents be open-minded. In a section entitled 'Temptations Faced by Pastoral Workers in the Church Today', Francis is blunt in his criticism of those who exhibit closed minds. 'A supposed soundness of doctrine or discipline', he writes, 'leads instead to a narcissistic and authoritarian elitism whereby, instead of evangelising, one analyses and classifies others'.

These teachings of Pope Francis provide a helpful introduction to the life and work of John Courtney Murray, who was one of the important Jesuits working in the intellectual ministry in the twentieth century. Murray lived in times when closed and rigid thinking prevailed in the Catholic Church, but he acted as an important prophet of open-minded thinking, eventually contributing significantly to that moment of reform in the Church, the Second Vatican Council.

The Early Years

John Courtney Murray, was born in 1904 in New York City. His father, Michael John Murray, was a lawyer who, together with his mother, Margaret Courtney, created a loving home for John and his siblings. John grew up as a well-adjusted, intelligent boy with a mischievous sense of humour. In later years, his nephews and nieces remember him as a loving uncle who liked to play golf, and was not averse to enjoying a dry martini with their parents.

Murray joined the Jesuit novitiate at the age of sixteen, beginning a long period of Jesuit formation. The wide-ranging process of this formation suited him well. After two years of novitiate, he was sent to Boston College where he earned both a Bachelor's and Master's degree in classics and philosophy. Next, we was sent to Manila, in the Philippines, where he taught Latin and English Literature to high-school students for three years. Returning to the United States, he undertook his preliminary studies in theology and was ordained priest in 1933. He was then sent to Rome to study for a doctorate in theology at the Pontifical Gregorian University, which he completed in 1937.

Murray's Jesuit formation helped him develop broader horizons than were normal for a Catholic of his time. The 1920s and 1930s were years when authorities in the Catholic Church were on the alert for any hint of 'modernism'. Theology professors were expected to teach directly from approved manuals that employed neo-scholastic reasoning, designed to prove the truth of the Catholic faith and to reject various errors of modern thought. Paradoxically, it was by moving to Rome, to the centre of the Church, that Murray had one his most mind-opening experiences.

This occurred not so much through his formal studies as through the pastoral work he undertook in his spare time with an organisation called Catholic Action. This movement involved university students and young professionals who wanted to engage as Catholics in the political life of Italy. Convinced that Italian democracy could benefit from the influence of Christian values, they managed to get around the official Catholic ruling which prohibited Catholics in Italy from engaging in the political affairs of what was a relatively anti-clerical state.

Return to the United States

When Murray returned to the United States, he was given a series of significant appointments by his provincial superior. In addition to teaching theology in a Jesuit seminary near New York, he was assigned to the editorial board of a new journal, *Theological Studies*, and at the same time he was appointed as a founding editor of a new magazine for educated lay Catholics, America. Despite Murray's complaint that these commitments were pulling him in too many directions, his provincial refused to lessen his responsibilities. In truth, this combination of activities helped him to stay in touch with the cultural 'signs of the times', while also posing new and relevant questions to academic theology. As a Catholic journalist, Murray drew on his experience of Catholic Action in Italy to ask what role the Catholic Church should be playing in society in his own country. He developed a three-fold answer to this question.

Murray's first insight arose from his admiration for the separation of Church and state as prescribed by the Constitution of the United States of America. He noted that the lack of direct political power on the part of any one religious denomination did not inhibit the practice of religion from flourishing, nor did it prevent religious voices from exercising an influence on public policy-making. He also noted, however, that for historical reasons the religious voices that were most influential tended to be Protestant.

In the second place, Murray became convinced that the early decades of the twentieth century had witnessed a dumbing down of public debate in the United States. He attributed this to a number of factors: the difficulty of understanding public policy in an increasingly complicated industrial society, a reduction in the quality of education at a popular level and a weakening of the quality of debate in the media, often under the influence of self-interested media moguls.

Murray's third insight was a paradoxical one. He believed that the Catholic Church was in a particularly strong position to help defend the more highly principled aspects of American culture. His reason for thinking this was related to the inherent conservatism of Catholic thought. He noted that Catholic theology, against the current tide, had held firm to principles from Greek and Roman philosophy. These taught that the well-being of the political order (the *polis*) was based on the virtues of its citizenry who should enter, in a spirit of friendship, into robust debate on matters of public policy. By contrast with such an approach, Murray felt that a good deal of Protestant thought had fallen victim to a secularising tendency which was ineffective in challenging the crass materialism of modern culture.

Challenged by his Critics

In the late 1930s and early 1940s, Murray set out to communicate his threefold insight, which he expressed mostly in a series of articles. He was soon confronted, however, with criticisms from agnostic and Protestant writers. These argued that Catholic thinkers did not enjoy the kind of credibility that qualified them to be taken seriously in the American public square. They noted in particular that that the official teaching of the Catholic Church did not respect some basic principles of modern democracy, above all, the separation of Church and state.

On reflection, Murray felt obliged to recognise that his critics had a point. He acknowledged that, according to the official Catholic teaching then current, Catholics were expected to work for the establishment of the Catholic faith as the official religion of the state while exercising official intolerance of other religions. Reflecting on the practical implications of this position, Murray came to recognise that a model of the situation promoted by this teaching did indeed exist: the dictatorial regime of General Franco in Spain.

All of this led Murray to shift his area of central intellectual concern. He began to see that he would need to argue for the Catholic Church to develop its thinking on the question of religious freedom. He decided that all further discussion of the public role of the Catholic Church in modern society must take second place to this.

Developing an Argument for Religious Freedom

In June 1945, Murray published an article in *Theological Studies* called 'Freedom of Religion: the Ethical Problem'. Using the categories of neo-scholastic reasoning, he presented an argument in favour of religious freedom. The article immediately drew criticism from some high-level American churchmen who had the ear of the prefect of the Holy Office in the Vatican, Cardinal Alfredo Ottaviani. They alleged that Murray was a modernist.

In the face of their criticism, Murray recognised that his argument had, in fact, been poorly expressed. Indeed, he became convinced that it was impossible to make a convincing argument in favour of religious freedom by using the categories of Neo-Scholasticism, as he had done. He concluded that 'nothing is more unhelpful than an abstract starting point', and set out to rethink his whole approach. In doing so, he arrived at a significant insight: that it is not enough merely to identify important questions that affect our times, it is also important to employ the right method when thinking about them. He remained convinced of the truth of this insight for the rest of his life.

For the next eight years Murray employed a historical approach in addressing the question of religious freedom. His research led him to conclude that the Church's position, then current, had not always been its teaching. He identified how, when tension had arisen between the Roman emperor and Pope Gelasius in the fifth century, the pope had been prompted to develop a theology of Church-state relations. Pope Gelasius articulated a principle of *dual powers*, which held that both the emperor and the pope received their authority — separately — from God. This implied that they should interact respectfully, recognising the mutual importance for society of both the temporal and the spiritual realms.

By way of contrast, Murray traced the emergence in subsequent centuries of an alternative theology of Church-state relations. He noted how theologians began to assert that all authority from God on earth passed through the pope, who wielded two swords, one of which was spiritual and the other temporal. Based on this theology, the authority of kings over their subjects was seen as delegated to them by the pope.

In analysing these different teachings, Murray suggested that the theory of two swords was misguided from its inception, since it involved constructing a theological principle out of what was merely an accident of historical necessity. He explained that the invasions of the Dark Ages had caused the social order in Europe to collapse, thereby creating a vacuum of political authority. He described how this vacuum drew the Church into exercising a political tutelage, with bishops and popes assuming positions of temporal power. He went on to suggest that the time had long since passed when such intervention was necessary, and that the time had come for the Church to return to a theology of dual authority.

On the basis of his research, Murray began to publish a series of articles in *Theological Studies* outlining his position. In these, he suggested that some of the statements of Pope Pius XII after the

Second World War had been so positive about the value of Western democracy that they implied the beginning of a shift back towards a Gelasian position on Church-state relations. It did not take long for a negative reaction to appear, however. The prefect of the Holy Office, Cardinal Ottaviani, recognised that Murray was proposing, not only novel conclusions about Church-state relations, but also a novel method of reasoning in theology, a historical method. In response to pressure from the Cardinal, Murray's Jesuit superiors blocked the publication of the final article in the series, and prohibited him from any further publishing or teaching on these matters. This prohibition would remain in place for ten years.

Broadening Philosophical Foundations

Murray was just one of many progressive Catholic theologians who were censured during those years. In truth, he suffered less than many of the others. The silencing of Murray became a cause célèbre in the United States, with the media declaring that this event proved that the Catholic Church was no friend of modern democracy. The uproar occasioned by the controversy had one effect that the Vatican had not anticipated: amongst the American bishops, even those who had not previously agreed with Murray now came to do so.

In the meantime, Murray became famous as the face of progressive Catholic thinking. He continued to write articles on 'safe' topics in political philosophy, avoiding any mention of religious freedom. In both *America* and *Theological Studies*, he published a series of articles about the positive qualities of the American proposition, and calling for a deepening of public debate in the United States. He made a collection of these articles, and published them in book form in 1960, under the title *We Hold These Truths*. The book became a bestseller, and led to Murray's portrait appearing on the cover of Time magazine on 12 December that year. About this time also, Murray was approached by staff members of presidential candidate John F. Kennedy, consulting him about speeches the candidate planned to make explaining why being Catholic need not preclude him from being president.

In a sense, Murray became famous in 1960 for ideas that he had already been holding since the 1940s. In addition to the uncontroversial ideas expressed in *We Hold These Truths*, however, he had been also been developing some further innovative ideas. He recognised that the argument for religious freedom touched on questions that ran deeper than a simple retrieval of the teaching of a pope from the fifth century. He came to see that it revealed a much deeper need: for Catholic theology to overcome its fear of modernism and engage with modern philosophy.

His awareness of this need was reinforced by reading the philosophical work of a friend of his, the Canadian Jesuit Bernard Lonergan. Lonergan, who had been publishing major articles in *Theological Studies*, in 1957 produced an 800-page masterwork, *Insight: A Study of Human Understanding*. Murray studied this work carefully, and by 1959 had begun to employ its basic ideas as a foundation for most of his own thought. From his reading, Murray grasped the significance of what Lonergan was proposing: that the key issue facing Catholic theology was, as the title of an article by Lonergan suggests, 'The Transition from a Classicist World View to Historical Mindedness'.

Murray and the Second Vatican Council

The next phase of Murray's life involved him getting swept up into the providential events of the Second Vatican Council (1962–65). Earlier, in 1958, Murray had witnessed the election of Pope John XXIII, noting with amazement that this pope had begun to make statements that were more radical than the ones for which he had been silenced years earlier. Then, in 1963, Pope John published a major encyclical, *Pacem in terris*, of which Murray subsequently wrote an analysis. Murray noted how Pope John stated that the Church could be understood as a historical process that exists in interaction with wider, secular society, with each side needing to learn from the other. He noted in particular that Pope John explicitly asserted that the Church needs to learn from the secular world regarding the value of notions such as modern democracy, political freedom, human rights and the separation of Church and state.

One might imagine that, with such a pope in office, Murray would have been quickly rehabilitated and invited to be a theological expert at the Council. The internal workings of the Church were more complicated than that, however, and by the time the Council opened, control of its agenda remained in the hands of Cardinal Ottaviani. When the American bishops requested that they bring Murray with them as a theological expert, their request was turned down.

As the first session of the council unfolded, however, the power formerly wielded by Cardinal Ottaviani was greatly weakened. A progressive majority of bishops took control of proceedings and prepared carefully for the second session of the council (1963–64). They produced an outline plan of sixteen documents that would be discussed by the council over the remaining sessions, with the American bishops making sure that the issue of religious freedom would be included. Murray was given his plane ticket to be a *peritus* – or expert – at the council from the second session onwards.

In fact, it was only in the fourth and final session of the council (1964–65) that the Declaration on Religious Freedom, *Dignitatis humanae,* was approved. The document met with considerable opposition right until the end. Members of a conservative minority correctly recognised that it constituted the most clear-cut example in the council of a development of doctrine. It was what Murray had been working towards for twenty years.

An Open-Minded but Fallible Jesuit

Murray had the good fortune to see his life-project come to fruition. The passing of the Declaration on Religious Freedom brought Murray acclaim in many circles, where he was recognised as its 'chief scribe'. The acclaim had hardly subsided when, to widespread shock, Murray died suddenly in 1967. It transpired that, since childhood, he had had an undiagnosed congenital heart condition. He was sixty-three years old.

Now, more than fifty years after his death, is an appropriate time to evaluate Murray's life and achievements. First of all, it needs to be said, in the spirit of Pope Francis, that John Courtney Murray was a fallible human being who was at his best when he was humbly learning from past mistakes. Above all, he was the kind of good Jesuit that Pope Francis characterises as an open-ended thinker.

At an intellectual level, Murray was at his best when addressing the issue of religious freedom and related issues about the need for high-quality debate on matters of public policy. Even here, however, some Catholic voices suggest that his admiration for the American constitution could benefit from further nuance. One author, Frederick G. Lawrence, in an article published in 1996, suggests that American culture's descent into materialism could not be completely divorced from the materialist rationalism of its founding fathers, such as Thomas Jefferson.

Furthermore, it must be admitted that when Murray was expressing opinions on issues outside of his area of competence, he could be less impressive. During the 1950s and 1960s he was sometimes consulted by the American bishops on major issues of the day. These included the civil rights movement for African-Americans and geo-political questions such as how to evaluate socialist governments in Western Europe. Murray's reflections on these issues do not stand the test of time. They show that, on certain issues, he shared the prejudices of his time and place.

Growth in Wisdom

Some commentators have noted that in the articles Murray wrote in the early 1950s – those which led to his silencing – some intemperate opinions about the narrow-mindedness of the Vatican authorities had been expressed. By contrast, a marked change of tone is evident in his contributions during the Second Vatican Council, even in the face of some intense and personal criticism during the tortuous debates about the drafts of *Dignitatis humanae*.

During the Summer of 1963 he was asked to write an article for circulation to the conciliar bishops, defending a draft of the document on religious freedom which had been largely written by him. The article he wrote is considered by some to his finest. In it, he avoided all rhetorical condemnation of his opponents. Rather, he outlined with scrupulous accuracy the arguments of those who criticised the draft. He then went on to present the arguments of those who favoured the document. Without condemning any individual, he noted that the conciliar debates had represented an 'abortive dialogue', because one side had not been listening to the other. He continued with this incisive statement, which reflects the influence Bernard Lonergan:

> This abortive dialogue seems to indicate where the real issue lies. The First and Second View do not confront each other as affirmation confronts negation. Their differences are at a deeper level indeed, at a level so deep that it would be difficult to go deeper. They represent *the contemporary clash between classicism and historical consciousness.*

After making this statement, Murray concluded calmly that it was the responsibility of the bishops to decide which argument they deemed to be more persuasive. In adopting this approach, Murray showed how he had grown in wisdom about how to conduct himself in situations of conflict.

Finally, it is obvious that Murray's premature death was a huge loss. He had found the Vatican Council to be a liberating experience. Having won his battle on the question of religious liberty, he had begun to turn to other questions. Above all, he wished to contribute to the debates about how the council could be implemented. On issues such as ecumenism, the relationship of lay people to bishops, and the theology of non-Christian religions, he wrote articles that exhibited the enthusiasm of a young man. It looked as if he was set to make further important contributions both to Catholic journalism and to Catholic theology.

Perhaps the moral of the story of his sudden demise can be found in the reflections of Pope Francis: we should not turn to single, high-profile individuals to do our thinking for us. It remains a task of all Christians to be open-ended thinkers, eager to mediate between the Gospel and the signs of the times.

PART FIVE

South America

~ 11 ~
Good News for Paraguay:
Roque González de Santa Cruz SJ (1576–1628)

Kevin O'Higgins SJ

I was privileged to be present at the canonisation of Roque González on 16 May 1988, having arrived in Paraguay two years earlier. Roque was canonised, along with his fellow Jesuit martyrs, Juan del Castillo and Alfonso Rodríguez, during a visit to Paraguay by Pope – now Saint – John Paul II. At that time, Paraguay had spent almost thirty-five years under the dark, suffocating shadow of a dictatorial military regime. The following year this same regime, which had seemed absolutely entrenched and unshakable, collapsed, opening the door to a more hopeful future for the country. It may not be too far-fetched to regard modern Paraguay's transition from despair to hope as the first post-canonisation miracle of St Roque González de Santa Cruz.

Priest and Jesuit

Roque González, Paraguay's first canonised saint, was born in Asunción in 1576. Ordained as a diocesan priest at just twenty-two years of age, he was assigned to a parish attached to the Cathedral in Asunción. Somewhat prophetically, his bishop at the time was Martín Ignacio de Loyola (1550–1608), a Franciscan friar who was an extraordinary missionary himself and who also happened to be a grand-nephew of the founder of the Society of Jesus.

Roque spent ten years in charge of the Cathedral parish, where he committed himself wholeheartedly to pastoral ministry, concerning himself especially with the evangelisation of the indigenous Guaraní people. Having declined the post of vicar general for the Asunción diocese, he decided to enter the Society of Jesus, in the hope of achieving greater scope for his missionary vocation.

The Jesuit Reductions

The first three Jesuits had arrived in Paraguay in 1588, among them an Irishman and native of Limerick, Thomas Field (1549–1625). During the following two decades, the number of Jesuits there remained small and their activities were largely exploratory and tentative. From the beginning, however, their efforts were primarily directed towards the native Guaraní people, rather than the town dwellers, who were mainly either European or 'Criollo' – Paraguayan-born descendents of Spanish settlers. The Jesuit Province of Paraguay, which had been formally created in 1607, shortly before Roque González joined its ranks, covered a vast area, comprising the territories of present-day Paraguay, Bolivia, Argentina, Uruguay and parts of Chile and Brazil.

Very early on, the Jesuits developed a novel method of pastoral activity through the creation of 'reductions' for the Guaraní. A reduction was a settlement where families and groups of indigenous people, previously dispersed over a wide area, were gathered together into larger centres. While the evangelisation of the people was the Jesuits' primary intention, the reductions also made it possible to provide adequate food and secure shelter for them, and introduce wide-ranging facilities, such as education, training in crafts and medical care. In addition, they served as an effective means of defending the Guaraní against the ever-present threat of aggression from Spanish and Portuguese colonists and slave-traders.

During the fifteen years that I spent in Paraguay, I had the opportunity to visit several of these reductions, and to spend brief periods living in two of them. The one that I found most awe-inspiring is named Trinidad. It lies in semi-ruins in a remote area of southern Paraguay, near the city of Encarnación. What took me completely by surprise was the sheer scale of the enterprise. The buildings that remain are all constructed with adobe, tinted pale red by the characteristic Paraguayan soil. Set against the background of tropical vegetation, first impressions are dramatic and breathtaking. The roofless shells of a large church and a college are at the heart of the complex. Nearby are the rooms once inhabited by the Jesuits. Then, fanning out from the centre, are the former homes of the Guaraní inhabitants and the workshops where they studied music and the arts, and practised carpentry and other crafts necessary for the maintenance of the community. Surrounding the complex are the lands that were used for agriculture. Standing in the middle of Trinidad, it was very easy to imagine how impressive something on this scale must have been four centuries ago.

Some reductions were so well organised and productive that they were able to engage in trade with the colonial towns and even export surplus produce to Europe. All told, about one hundred reductions were established, with a total population, at the height of their flourishing, of close to 150,000 inhabitants. The project endured, more successfully in some places than others, for over 150 years.

One eighteenth-century Jesuit writer, José Manuel Peramás, suggested that the reductions were inspired, in part, by Plato's sketch of an ideal republic. Others have detected similarities with Thomas More's semi-satirical prescription for a utopian society or Tomasso Campanella's *City of the Sun.* Later writers, from the late nineteenth century right up to the present, have even portrayed the reductions as an experiment in communistic living that foreshadowed Marx's vision of an egalitarian society. It seems most unlikely that Roque González and his missionary companions would have had the time or leisure to indulge in utopian fantasies of any kind. In reality, the reductions were a pragmatic solution to a pressing problem, and were based on earlier Franciscan prototypes. Philip Caraman's study, *The Lost Paradise: the Jesuit Republic of South America*, offers a balanced account of the rise and eventual fall of this extraordinary experiment.

The Collapse of the Venture

Roland Joffé's famous film, *The Mission*, gives a broad idea of how a typical reduction functioned, and the close connection that was fostered between the Jesuits and the Guaraní people in its structure and governance. It also highlights the disputes that, inevitably, pitted the Jesuits and the Guaraní against powerful outside forces, whose main concern was to exploit the labour of the people and the wealth of the land. In the dilemma that is at the centre of the film, one of the main Jesuit protagonists focuses on the spiritual dimension of their task, while the other feels compelled to address the immediate threat posed by hostile political and commercial interests. Roque González experienced these same tensions in his own missionary endeavours. He was intensely committed to the spiritual welfare of the Guaraní, but he saw this commitment as inseparable from his efforts to protect them from exploitation and to improve their lives in more immediate ways. In the end, it was mounting political tensions in Europe that led to the expulsion of the Jesuits from all Spanish Crown territories in 1767, giving rise eventually, six years later, to the suppression of the Society of Jesus by Pope Clement XIV.

Most of the reductions collapsed with the expulsion of the Jesuits, although a small number did survive more or less intact. Some of them later grew into small towns, and several eventually evolved to become present-day cities in Paraguay and neighbouring countries. Today, some of the original constructions are being maintained by Jesuit communities, usually as parishes or spirituality centres, while others have been restored as tourist attractions. Many have been recognised by UNESCO as World Heritage Sites.

The Central Role of Roque González

The story of the reductions forms the backdrop for Roque Gonzalez's entire missionary enterprise. In 1612, he was sent by his provincial to evangelise the area bordering the vast Paraná river, which stretches 4,880 kilometres through present-day Brazil, Paraguay and Argentina. Roque set about this task with enthusiasm, and within six years he had founded three reductions, adding a further seven during the following decade. That is the equivalent of planning, constructing and inaugurating ten brand new towns in the space of just sixteen years, an extraordinary achievement in itself.

In many of his letters to the provincial in Asunción, Roque describes the hardships he endured in the course of his missionary journeys. Arriving for the first time in a remote location, with practically no possessions, the first challenge was merely to survive. Often, this meant constructing a precarious shelter from whatever materials were readily available. Soon afterwards, a rudimentary chapel was usually added. Food frequently consisted of an involuntary vegetarian diet of maize, cassava – a shrub-like plant rich in carbohydrates – and tropical herbs that were found in abundance and are still the preferred remedy for all manner of ailments among many Paraguayans.

The next challenge facing González was to convince local Guaraní leaders that living closer together in a reduction offered them the best prospect for improving the lives of their people and protecting them from the colonists who were encroaching on their territory and threatening their freedom. Particularly painful to the Guaraní was the *encomienda* system, which governed their relations with the colonists. This was a system whereby, by royal decree, colonists were given the right to extract both tribute – usually in the form of food – and forced labour from indigenous people. From the outset, Roque and the other Jesuits working in the reductions fiercely opposed this system. Not surprisingly, their opposition earned them many enemies among those who were enriching themselves at the expense of the Guaraní, known as *encomenderos*.

On more than one occasion, González had to defend himself against false rumours and accusations that the Jesuits were preparing the Guaraní for an armed insurrection against the Spanish Crown. In a letter written in 1614 to his brother, Francisco, who was then governor of Asunción, Roque tells him that it was an honour to be the object of such calumnies, because the cause of defending the Guaraní was noble and just.

> Our Lord, who sees and knows everything, will send a remedy, and when the time comes to reward service and goodness ... he will punish offenses, particularly against the poor ... I hope you can see how the colonists have misinformed you, claiming that the Indians owe them years of tribute. This has astonished me, because I know that, even if they were left with just the shirts on their backs, they could never repay the debt they owe to the Indians. The blindness of the *encomenderos* is so great that anyone who knows and fears God will refuse to hear their confession. Nor will I confess anyone, however powerful, who refuses to acknowledge that he has done wrong, never mind being willing to make amends.

Establishing trust with the Guaraní was essential, since adapting to life in a reduction meant an enormous cultural change, and success was only possible with the willing cooperation of the Guaraní themselves. In most of the reductions, just two or three Jesuits lived with as many as a thousand indigenous families. Roque quickly established a pattern in establishing a new reduction. He would arrive alone, or sometimes with one or two companions, into a previously unexplored area. After an initial period of a few months, during which he became acquainted with the area and the local Guaraní leaders, he would start to construct a small chapel and, perhaps, a school and some houses. He would then write to the provincial in Asunción asking for additional Jesuits, whose task it would be to build on the foundations already in place. Once these new Jesuits had arrived and the project appeared to be on a reasonably firm footing, Roque would move on in search of a site for another new reduction.

From his own letters and other contemporary documents, we get a good picture of Roque's character, faults and all. The impression that emerges is of a man constantly on the move, always looking to the next project, unsparing in the demands he made of himself and others. In a letter to the Jesuit general, Mutio Vitelleschi, the Paraguayan provincial observes that Roque is an excellent missionary with a gift for languages, although not suited to academic work and inclined to be somewhat melancholic. He adds that Roque's fellow Jesuits see him as prudent, of sound judgement and a good leader. In response, Fr Vitelleschi suggests that the provincial should advise Roque to be less scrupulous and more affable in his dealings with Jesuit companions. It is reassuring to know that Roque, like most saintly individuals, had some normal human limitations. Nevertheless, these pale in comparison with his extraordinary single-mindedness in fulfilling the mission entrusted to him.

Martyrdom

After sixteen years of intensive missionary work, tirelessly travelling from one remote location to another and establishing new reductions along the way, Roque González died a martyr on 15 November 15 1628, along with his Spanish-born Jesuit companion, Alonso Rodríguez. Two days later, another Spanish Jesuit, Juan del Castillo, met the same fate. All three were in the process of establishing a new reduction in Caaró, which is in the south of modern Brazil. Ironically, after so many years defending the Guaraní against the Spanish colonists, Roque's death was instigated, not by the *encomenderos*, but by a Guaraní shaman – a type of medicine man – who regarded the arrival of the Jesuits as a threat to his own authority and prestige. Roque was killed as he was installing a bell outside a newly constructed chapel. According to contemporary accounts, he died instantly after being struck on the head with an axe. Following his death, the chapel was set alight and his body was thrown into the flames.

These accounts also relate that when some Guaraní from a nearby reduction went to recover the remains of the three slain Jesuits, they were surprised to find that Roque's heart had survived the fire. Together with other relics, including the axe with which Roque was killed, his heart was eventually transported to Rome, where it remained in the Gesú, the principal Jesuit Church there, for many years. In 1928, these relics were moved to Buenos Aires, and later, in 1968, at the request of Jesuit superior general Pedro Arrupe, they were returned to his birthplace, Asunción. For the past fifty years they have been objects of veneration in the chapel attached to the Jesuits' Cristo Rey College in Asunción. When Pope Francis visited Paraguay in 2015, he spent some time kneeling in prayer before the reliquary containing the heart of Roque González.

Influence Today

To modern eyes, the reductions may seem overly idealistic, and some people have criticised them as being paternalistic. The Jesuit project, like most missionary enterprises of that era, could not avoid being tinged with some ambiguities arising from the links between evangelisation and European colonial expansion. Nevertheless, it is undoubtedly true that the reductions were instrumental, not only in spreading the gospel among the indigenous population, but also in preserving their dignity and protecting them from marauding colonists. Their opposition to the encomienda system and the success of many of the reductions frequently made enemies of the Jesuits among the colonists. Unlike the experience of most indigenous ethnic groups during the same period, the Guaraní population increased and their language and culture were preserved to an extent not seen elsewhere in America, North or South.

Even today, Paraguay is officially bilingual, with most people preferring to speak Guaraní rather than Spanish in ordinary, everyday conversation. Paraguay's unit of currency is named after the Guaraní, and a portrait of Roque González adorns the ₲100,000 banknote – worth about fifteen euro. One of the main bridges linking Paraguay and Argentina is named after Roque, while another honours St Ignatius Loyola. Throughout Paraguay, there are constant reminders of what was one of the most extraordinary and creative enterprises in the Church's missionary history. At the centre of that enterprise was the inspiring figure of St Roque González.

~ 12 ~

Tireless in Service:
Alberto Hurtado SJ (1901–1952)

Fergus O'Donoghue SJ

Alberto Hurtado lived for less than fifty-two years, but his life and his legacy are fundamental to the development of a renewed Catholicism in Latin America. He was ahead of his time, both in his thinking and in his apostolic activity, and his life story fits into the ongoing tension between the conservative and progressive tendencies in the Latin American Church. Alberto had such a keen appreciation of the needs of the poor and of the ways in which they could be helped that we can now see him as a forerunner of Liberation Theology. Pope Francis, who urges priests to be 'shepherds with the smell of the sheep', has found inspiration in Alberto's example.

Early Years

Alberto's father and mother, Alberto Hurtado and Ana Cruchaga, were a very united couple, of Spanish Basque ancestry. They were living in the city of Viña del Mar, in Chile, when their first child was born, on 22 January 1901. They named him Alberto, after his father. A second son, Miguel, was born two years later. Not long afterwards, however, tragedy struck the family and disrupted their settled lives.

Young Alberto was only four years old, and Miguel still a toddler, when their father died in a violent incident.

Ana, now a young widow, was in shock from her sudden loss. In the absence of good advice, she decided to sell the extensive family property in order to pay her debts, and moved with her little family to the capital, Santiago. There they were able to live with relatives, but found they often had to move. From this experience, they knew all the bitterness and humiliation that comes with being the 'poor relations'. Nevertheless, despite all the hardships involved, Ana concentrated on the upbringing of her two children, encouraging them to grow up as good Christians and never to harbour resentment.

At the age of eight, Alberto was accepted on a scholarship to the Jesuit school in Santiago, Colegio San Ignacio, where he proved himself to be a clever student. From there he went on to study law at the Catholic University of Chile. During his student years, in order to help his mother and brother, he worked in the afternoons and evenings for a Catholic newspaper and a political party.

While anticlerical and Catholic groups were constantly opposed to each other in Chile, the country had a very strong democratic tradition. Having grown up in poverty and insecurity, Alberto always felt close to the poor and, even as a schoolboy, spent his Sunday afternoons visiting and helping them. It comes as a surprise, then, to discover that young Alberto was politically very conservative. He worked for a conservative magazine and joined a conservative party. This is even more surprising in the light of his later priestly work.

Jesuits in Chile

Chile is the longest country in the world, stretching 4,300 kilometres from the northern deserts to the Antarctic wastes. It is also a very narrow country: at its widest, it measures only 350 kilometres. Originally a Spanish colony, Chile became an independent republic in 1818 and preserved its democratic traditions for generations. It was a healthy democracy in Alberto's lifetime, but it was marred by much social inequality.

Jesuits first arrived in Chile in 1593. They founded a strong educational apostolate, and also worked closely with indigenous peoples, whose languages they learned. The Chilean Jesuits lived very simply, but their land holdings made them seem quite rich to some people, and this provoked enmity and greed. In 1767, King Charles III of Spain expelled all Jesuits from Spain and the Spanish Empire, with the consequence that all of the 181 Jesuits then in Chile were deported to Italy.

When another king eventually permitted the Jesuis to return to Chile in 1816, almost forty years later, only six of the expelled group were still alive. Two years after the return of the Jesuits Chile declared its independence from Spain. The Jesuits in Chile now concentrated on working in towns and cities, paying special attention to the new urban poor, whose numbers kept increasing as people left the countryside.

Years of Formation
Alberto finished his military service and qualified as a lawyer in 1923. Since his family no longer needed his financial help at that time, he decided, with his mother's blessing, to enter the Society of Jesus that same year. The Jesuit formation he received was rigorous, beginning with two years of novitiate. Along with the other first-year novices, Alberto made a thirty-day retreat, based on the Spiritual Exercises of St Ignatius Loyola, early in his novitiate. After first vows, he continued his training in Argentina, before going to Spain, to study philosophy and theology in Barcelona. When the new Spanish Republic declared the Jesuits illegal, Alberto moved to Belgium, where he was ordained in Louvain on 24 August 1933.

At that point, the Chilean Department of Education invited Alberto to study European teaching methods. His research, carried out in Belgium, Holland, France and Germany, earned him a doctorate in 1935. He remained in Belgium for the final period of his Jesuit formation – Tertianship – when he made the Spiritual Exercises for the second time. It is worth noting that, while in Europe he visited Ireland for a time, where he stayed with the Jesuits at Rathfarnham Castle, Dublin.

Returning to Chile in 1936, Alberto brought back with him with a wide variety of experiences, as well as an international outlook that would always be a source of inspiration to him and to others. He had a broad mind that was interested in everything, and never seemed to be bored by anything or anybody. His years in Europe also a brought him to experience directly the rise of fascism, and made him aware of the threat from communism. All of this influenced his work for the next sixteen years of his life.

Educator and Preacher

Back at his old school, Colegio San Ignacio, Alberto proved himself to be a very successful teacher. He used to say, 'It's much easier to teach than to educate', so he set about giving his students the broadest and deepest education he could. As a teacher of religion and as spiritual director of the Boys' Sodality, he enthusiastically encouraged vocations to the priesthood.

In 1938, he was given the task of building a new novitiate for the Chilean Jesuits who, until then, had been a mission dependent on Spain. Since this task included the raising of funds for the project, Alberto had the idea of also building a retreat house next to the novitiate. This proposal was approved, and when it was finished, he himself gave retreats there whenever he could. This retreat house is now named after him.

Alberto was a very successful preacher. As can be heard from the few sermons that are available on the internet, he had a high, clear voice, never used long sentences, and was very direct in everything he said. Listening to one of his sermons, 'Una Homilia del Padre Alberto Hurtado', which lasts almost fourteen minutes, the very tone of his voice conveys his optimism and his love for God and the people. Indeed, love was Alberto's principal theme, summed up in his saying, 'We are put into this world to love and be loved'. He held that a smile costs us nothing, but it is one of the greatest gifts we can give.

Catholic Youth Groups

In 1941, Alberto wrote a sensational book called *Is Chile a Catholic Country?* in which he questioned the social principles of the Chilean Church. Soon afterwards, he was made national chaplain of the youth branch of the Catholic Action Movement, many of whose members were university students. Alberto, with his aim of 'forming the man, forming the Christian, and forming the leader', wanted them to immerse themselves in the real world. His impact was astonishing. Within three years, membership rose from 1,500 to 12,000.

By then, Alberto had formed another youth group, called 'The Service of Christ the King'. Committed to voluntary social work, its members were enrolled in a solemn ceremong for one year of fulltime service. While many people were captivated by Alberto's extraordinary charity and by his ability to try something new, nevertheless the speed with which he did everything was disturbing to those with less imagination. Opposition to his youth work meant that Alberto had to leave it in November 1944.

Just a month earlier, while giving a retreat to a group of women, he spoke about how he had met a hungry and homeless beggar in the street. 'Each one of those men is Christ,' he proclaimed, 'and what have we done for them?' Those present were so impressed that they gave generous donations, including land, to provide help to those most in need.

Hogar de Cristo

The foundation stone of the first *Hogar de Cristo* ('Hearth of Christ' or 'Home of Christ') was laid on 21 December 1944, near Santiago's central railway station. It was to be a place of refuge for the homeless. In 1945, he opened a home for street children, whom he had seen living under a bridge in Santiago and, in 1946, Alberto founded a school that would not only teach basic literacy to these children, but would also teach them a trade, thereby enabling them to earn a living.

Alberto had visited Fr Edward Flanagan's famous Boys Town in

Nebraska, and he now adopted its methods. He would go out in a small green lorry, collect the homeless children, and bring them to their new home. There they were given a good meal and a clean bed, often for the first time in their lives. Within six years, 846,000 children had been helped in this way. Initially, the Chilean bishops were suspicious of these developments, wondering if they might be a front for communism. Eventually, as we shall see, they gave their approval in 1950.

Chilean Trade Union Association

Alberto was tireless in his concern for the poorer section of society. His next idea was to work closely with the trade unions, and in 1947, despite the reservations of the Chilean bishops, he founded the Chilean Trade Union Association. That same year he went to Europe and was warmly received by Pope Pius XII. From him he received a precious gift: his blessing on the proposal to educate trade unionists and young employers in Catholic social teaching. Alberto had come to realise that going to the top and getting papal approval was the only way to overcome the local opposition he was experiencing.

Alberto had a saying, 'It is in his work that the worker is sanctified', and to elaborate his position he published three influential books about Catholic social teaching. In 1950, he published an important book on *Christian Social Order in the Documents of the Hierarchy and Trade Unionism: History, Theory and Practice*.

A New Monthly Journal

The need to spread an understanding of the Church's social teaching inspired Alberto still further. He founded a new monthly journal *Mensaje* ('Message') in October 1951. This was year after he had he had won the support of the Chilean hierarchy, whose approval was a very important moment in his life. Opposition to Alberto's actions was growing among some conservative Catholics, who were calling him 'The Red priest'. In their opinion, any support of trade unions and of the rights of workers was the first step towards communism.

In those early years of the Cold War, when the Church was enduring terrible persecution in communist countries, such an allegation was taken very seriously by many. Indeed, some Chilean Catholics had been very reluctant to accept Catholic social teaching, which had begun with the encyclical letter *Rerum novarum* of Pope Leo XIII in 1891, and which had been reinforced and developed by Pope Pius XI in his encyclical of 1931, *Quadragesimo anno*. Alberto vigorously defended the Church's teaching on social issues and constantly looked for opportunities to put it into action in tangible ways. It became central to Chilean Catholic life.

A Flourishing legacy

For some time, Alberto had been ignoring the abdominal pain he been increasingly experiencing. He waited until it became very severe to attend to it, and by that stage the condition was very bad and the diagnosis too late. By 1952, it was obvious that Alberto was dying of pancreatic cancer, a form of the disease that still remains very difficult to treat. Alberto's suffering was made worse by the absence of palliative care, an approach that was developed only later. Despite the dreadful pain he endured, he willingly met all those who came to see him. Dying in the prime of life, Alberto wanted everybody to know that he was at peace. 'I am happy, Lord, I am happy,' he would say, 'because I am returning to God, my Father'.

Alberto Hurtado died on 18 August 1952, but his legacy still continues strongly today, over sixty years later. All the apostolates he founded continue to flourish to this day. The *Hogares de Cristo* continues under Jesuit direction in over 500 centres, giving help to some 25,000 very needy people every month. Alberto's work with youth has meant that the Chilean Province of the Society of Jesus has never lacked vocations. In 1997, when the Chilean Jesuits merged three third-level institutes into one body, they named the new institute Universidad Alberto Hurtado after their inspirational colleague.

Alberto was regarded as a saint in his own lifetime, not least because of his amazing optimism and joyfulness. His work for the poor and for youth won him a national reputation, so that his death was followed by immediate devotion to him among the faithful. Civil society also recognised his enormous contribution and the Chilean parliament made the anniversary of his death an annual Day of National Solidarity.

With the beatification of Alberto Hurtado by Pope John Paul II on 16 October 1994, work on the construction of a new shrine began at once, and his remains were moved there in the following year. The shrine, which is situated in the noisy and busy centre of Santiago close to the central station where the first *Hogar de Cristo* was established, is now a place of silence and prayer. A small museum, telling the story of Alberto's life, work and ideals, was subsequently built beside the shrine. He continues to be a source of inspiration and hope for the people of Chile.

Alberto Hurtado was canonised by Pope Benedict XVI, along with four others, at the closing Mass of the Synod on the Eucharist on 23 October 2005.

~ 13 ~
At the Service of the Poor:
José María Vélaz SJ (1910–85)

Kevin O'Higgins SJ

Fe y Alegría is the name of one of the most extraordinary educational projects ever conceived. Its title – which translates as 'Faith and Joy'– makes clear from the start the two pillars on which it is based. Founded in Venezuela in 1954, it has since expanded into twenty-one countries throughout Latin America, as well as to Africa, the Caribbean and Europe. Currently, it has over 1,500 schools, institutes and other educational centres, with approximately 1.6 million students. That is an extraordinary achievement in itself. What makes it all the more extraordinary is the fact that Fe y Alegría is dedicated exclusively to offering quality education to the poorest of the poor, especially those living in urban slums and remote rural areas neglected by national governments. 'Education for the poor must not be poor education' is one of the mottos of Fe y Alegría, and indeed multiple studies have shown that students in Fe y Alegría schools frequently achieve better academic results than their counterparts in state-run and other school systems.

Founded on Generosity and Sacrifice
To understand how such an amazing project came into being, it

is necessary to focus on its founder, the Chilean-born Jesuit José María Vélaz (1910–1985). Vélaz himself would be the first to insist, however, that while he may have founded Fe y Alegría, his ideas could never have been translated into reality without the help of some truly exceptional friends and allies. In fact, the very first school was made possible only through the extraordinary generosity and selflessness of a poor family living in Caracas, the capital of Venezuela.

Abraham and Patricia Reyes had spent years building a modest home for themselves and their eight children in a poor suburb of the city. When they heard that Vélaz was desperately searching for a building in which to start a school, such was their passionate belief in the importance of education as a way out of poverty and marginalisation that they immediately offered part of their own small home to him for the project. The history of Fe y Alegría is replete with similar stories of generosity and sacrifice.

Early Years

For José María Vélaz, the story began in Chile, where he was the first-born child of José and Josefina Vélaz. His father died when he was just five years old, leaving the family in a financially precarious situation. Having nowhere else to turn, his mother decided that they would move to Spain, to a small town in the north of the country, where she had relatives capable of supporting her young family. This move was providential for José María, for the small town was Loyola, the birthplace of St Ignatius, the founder of the Jesuits. Given the strong devotion to St Ignatius in that part of the world, it is not surprising that José María soon found himself in a Jesuit boarding school. From there, he went to university to study law, but after two years he was convinced that his real vocation lay elsewhere.

He entered the Society of Jesus in 1928. The years preceding the civil war in Spain were tumultuous, with the Church caught up in the confrontation between monarchists and republicans. In view of the confusion and dangers of the time, José María, along with his fellow Jesuit students, was sent to Belgium for the initial stages of his training. During this time, he developed a desire to go to China as part of his formation as a Jesuit, but that was not to be. In 1936, instead of China, he was told in a letter from his provincial that he was destined to go to Venezuela. In later life, he admitted that his heart had been so set on working in China that he found it hard initially to muster much enthusiasm for his new mission. Once there, however, he found himself falling in love with Venezuela and its people. He spent four years teaching in a large secondary school in Caracas, before returning to Spain to complete his theological studies, He was ordained a priest in 1943, and returned to Venezuela in 1946.

After several years as a teacher and rector of a large boarding school, Vélaz requested that he be allowed to begin work on a new agricultural college for young people in a neglected rural area. His request was turned down, and his Provincial sent him instead to teach in the Jesuit university in Caracas. This decision may have been prompted by the fact that evaluations of his time in charge of the boarding school had been quite critical, with some people saying that he was temperamentally unsuited to direct any sizeable project. How wrong they were! Before long, Vélaz would find himself directing, not just one school, but the biggest educational project anywhere in the world.

A Providential Beginning

Vélaz began work at the Andrés Bello University in 1954 with an assignment to teach classes in religious studies. He was also appointed chaplain to the Marian Congregation, a world-wide association of Catholic students that was devotional in character, but also committed to charitable work with the poor. This latter assignment turned out to be even more providentially decisive than his original posting to Venezuela. Accompanying groups of students on their visits to some of the worst slum areas of Caracas, Vélaz could see immediately that there was an obvious link between the appalling poverty he found and the high levels of illiteracy in the community. By the end of his first year in the university, he had launched an initial attempt at addressing this situation, and had begun to consider the possibility of opening a school for the children living in the slum.

That was when he met Abraham and Patricia Reyes, who offered him the use of their modest house. The house had been under construction for about seven years. Whenever money became available, Abraham bought additional bricks and cement, and when there was no money, he was prepared to wait patiently. By the time the couple met José María Vélaz, a second floor had been added. Hearing of Vélaz's hopes for the area, Abraham and Patricia urged him to accept this top floor for his project, while they and their eight children would continue to live underneath. That experience of generous giving had a tremendous impact on Vélaz. He used to say that the extraordinary self-sacrifice of the Reyes family helped him to understand the essence of his Christian faith more than all his years studying theology.

Like the Mustard Seed

The first Fe y Alegría primary school was opened in March 1955, with an intake of 175 pupils. The teaching staff were local young adults, most of whom had themselves never had the opportunity to advance beyond primary education. It was a daunting task, but Vélaz insisted that, however much the odds might seem to be stacked against them, the enterprise would always be joyful if it was motivated by faith in God and other people. Faith and joy, he came to see, would be its hallmark.

The quick growth of Fe y Alegría was living proof that Vélaz's optimism was not fanciful. Once the first school was up and running, he began to receive donations from acquaintances and former students in support of his efforts, and additional money was raised through fund-raising campaigns. In less than a year, he was able to improve facilities in the first school and add a new one, this time catering for 900 secondary students.

From that point on, Fe y Alegría began to receive a lot of positive media publicity. Financial support began to pour in from all quarters, and offers of help from political, business and other sectors quickly followed. By 1960, there were five schools in operation, catering for over 6,000 students. Subsequently, the project expanded rapidly throughout Venezuela and beyond; it also became more diversified, with schools and training centres offering programmes to all age groups, from early childhood to mature adulthood.

As time went on, as well as educational programmes Fe y Alegría centres began to organise food programmes, medical assistance and even holiday camps for children from poor areas. By the end of the 1960s, the project was established in six countries, and from then on it continued to expand beyond anyone's expectations throughout the countries of Latin America and into Africa and Europe. Like the mustard seed in the gospel parable, from the smallest beginnings Fe y Alegría became an enormous tree, with many branches, and bearing much fruit.

Tenderness and Stubbornness Combined

People who worked closely with José María Vélaz and knew him best speak of his unshakeable faith in God's providence. His constant advice to anyone worried about trying to achieve too much was, 'Take a risk!' He was never one to play by anyone else's rules, because for him it was always a matter of prioritising the needs of the poor, however large their numbers or pressing their problems. When the Venezuelan government eventually recognised the enormous importance of Fe y Alegría and agreed to help with construction costs and salaries, Vélaz urged his teachers not to pay too much attention to bureaucratic regulations about class sizes or curriculum content. For him, the concrete needs of the poor were paramount. His friends also speak about how he combined extraordinary tenderness, when dealing with people in need, with a dogged stubbornness whenever obstacles – especially those arising from officialdom – threatened to frustrate his plans. At times, his frustration led to explosive outbursts but, as one close friend pointed out, 'He had to be like that. How else could he have achieved so much?'

There were some signs early on that the pace and intensity of his work with Fe y Alegría was taking a toll on his health. Vélaz suffered a mild cardiac arrest in 1964 from which he recovered, but later, in 1973, he had to undergo open-heart surgery. Far from slowing down, however, he continued to direct the expanding network of Fe y Algería with unflagging energy, and he even began to explore new ways of making education available to still greater numbers of people. With this in mind, he launched a new educational project by radio in the mid-1970s. This proved to be a huge success and is still going strongly, especially in Bolivia, Ecuador, Paraguay, Peru and Venezuela. Offering education to all age groups, especially adults who missed out on early education, it works by combining the study of texts with radio tutorials and weekly meetings with tutors in designated centres.

Final Years

While Fe y Alegría continued to expand beyond anyone's expectations, ill health and advancing years began to have their effect on Vélaz, making it impossible for him to carry on as before. He became painfully aware that, even within Fe y Alegría itself, some people believed that it was time for him to step aside and allow others to assume overall direction of the project. Eventually, he recognised himself that that was the right thing to do, and in 1976 he relinquished his role as director of the immense project.

He found the sudden change extremely difficult, even as he believed that it was necessary for the sake of the work he had begun. Initially, on retiring, he opted to live alone in a remote rural area, where his isolation was almost complete, the nearest public telephone being about 90 kilometres away. During those days of withdrawal, he spent his time in a kind of retreat, thinking, writing and praying.

As time went on, public recognition of his monumental achievements came in the form of academic and civic awards, but he was never one to rest on his achievements. Even in retirement, he was still thinking of what remained to be done, and he set his mind on one final project. His period of isolation had made him acutely aware of the needs of young people living in remote rural areas, many of them condemned to dire poverty. His final initiative was the establishment of a major agricultural college, San Javier del Valle Grande. It was as if the project he had dreamt of nearly thirty years earlier had at last come true. Founded in 1977, San Javier is still operating, with about 500 students from a rural or indigenous background, most of whom are boarders. Currently, it offers training in a wide range of technical subjects.

Faith in Providence

The extraordinary life of José María Vélaz reached the end of its earthly phase on 18 June 1985. Among his papers was a written testament, later to be published, to the faith that inspired him to undertake the brave initiative that he eventually called Fe y Alegría:

> It took me a long time to settle on the name Fe y Alegría, and I spent many hours thinking about it. I found the word 'faith' attractive, because it summed up a lot of abstract ideas that I wanted to make real and alive: faith in God, in his love, his grandeur, his providence, his wisdom, his eternity, his forgiveness and mercy; faith in Christ, in his incarnation, his humble life, his divinity, his power, his infinitely loving heart, his Eucharistic sacrifice and resurrection; faith in the Church, the mystery of salvation, the continuation of Christ's presence in the world and in history; faith in the transcendent destiny of all human beings; faith in human values, in the capacity for love and intelligence ... I always believed that people of faith are full of hope and love, that nothing raises up life more than faith.

Holiness comes in many guises, as many as there are holy people. José María Vélaz probably never thought of himself as being particularly holy or saintly, but he surely was. His actions and his tenacity were rooted in a hidden life of faith and prayer, leading to an unshakable confidence in the providence of God, who would show him the way and give him the courage he needed, whatever the obstacle.

His early life was completely ordinary and unremarkable. Yet, in the light of what came later, it is clear that, if even a few details had been different, Fe y Alegría and his other initiatives would never have happened. If his father had not died when he did, the young José María would not have travelled to Loyola, and would probably not have become a Jesuit. If his provincial had sent him to China rather than Venezuela, or if the young Jesuit had resisted being sent to work in the university, or if he hadn't met Patricia and Abraham Reyes, the chain of events that led to the launch of Fe y Alegría would never have happened. José María Valéz was well aware that the most significant turning points in his life all happened, not through his own choosing, but through the mysterious action of God. When he wrote about trusting in God's loving providence, his primary point of reference was the surely the amazing story of his own life.

~ 14 ~

A Mysticism of Open Eyes:
Ignacio Ellacuría SJ (1930–1989)

Michael O'Sullivan SJ

It was dangerous to be a Jesuit in Latin America after 1968. That was the year the Latin American Catholic Bishops Conference (CELAM) met at Medellín, Colombia, and declared that the historical direction of salvation in Jesus Christ embraced the continent's struggle for liberation from political and economic oppression. God's salvation, the bishops taught, is an integral reality with many dimensions. Because it is historical, it is mediated through a faith-filled reading of how God is at work in the signs of the times.

> We have undertaken to discover a plan of God in the 'signs of the times'. We interpret the aspirations and clamours of Latin America as signs that reveal the direction of the divine plan operating in the redeeming love of Christ … It appears to be a time full of zeal for full emancipation, of liberation from every form of servitude … As Christians we believe that this historical stage of Latin America is intimately linked to the history of salvation.

CELAM identified the commitment to liberation as a vocation that could even lead to martyrdom: 'By its own vocation,' they stated, 'Latin America will undertake its liberation at the cost of whatever sacrifice'.

Just over twenty years later, on 16 November 1989, six Jesuits made the ultimate sacrifice, when soldiers of the Atlacatl battalion, who had been trained in the United States, broke into the home of the community of the Jesuit University in San Salvador. They proceeded to murder Ignacio Ellacuría and his five Jesuit companions and, in order to leave no witnesses, they also murdered their housekeeper and her teenage daughter.

Ellacuría as Rector of UCA

Ellacuría was the rector – president, in US terms – of the university. It was named in honour of Fr José Simeón Cañas, who had brought an end to slavery in Central America in 1824, forty years before Lincoln did so in the United States. The more common name for the university, however, is University of Central America (UCA).

Ellacuría had been rector for almost ten years by the time of his murder. During those years he had transformed the university so that it would effectively promote 'liberation from servitude'. In pursuing this goal, he was not content with using the university as a platform for addressing the suffering of the great majority of the Salvadoran people. Going far beyond that, he dedicated himself to ensuring that the normal functions of a university – research, teaching, public lectures, publications and what he called 'social projection' – were imbued with and inspired by genuine Christian faith and love, aimed at bringing good news to the poor and setting the oppressed free (Lk 4:16–20). He expressed his vision clearly in 1982:

> We should always look at our own peculiar historical reality
> … The university must carry out this general commitment
> with the means uniquely at its disposal: we as an intellectual
> community must analyse causes; use imagination and
> creativity together to discover remedies; communicate to our

constituencies a consciousness that inspires the freedom of self-determination; educate professionals with a conscience, who will be the immediate instruments of such a transformation; and continually hone an educational institution that is academically excellent and ethically oriented.

Ellacuría then elaborated on how he saw a Christian university:

A Christian university must take into account the gospel preference for the poor. This does not mean that only the poor study at the university; it does not mean that the university should abdicate its mission of academic excellence, excellence needed in order to solve complex problems ... It does mean that the university should be present intellectually where it is needed: to give intellectual support for those who do not possess the academic qualifications to promote and legitimate their rights.

His aim was to transform the normal functions of a university into liberating functions, contributing to what he called 'the liberation of the Salvadoran people'. This approach would enable them to address what in 1986 he called 'the original violence of structural injustice in the country, which violently maintains through economic, social, political and cultural structures, the majority of the population in a situation of permanent violation of their human rights'. To those who claimed that such an approach would compromise the academic rigour and independence expected of a university, Ellacuría responded unambiguously: 'The university should strive to be free and objective, but objectivity and freedom may demand taking sides'. He was quite clear that the University of Central America took the side of the poor 'because they are unjustly oppressed'.

Background to his Stance
Ellacuría's position on objectivity was influenced, not only by his lived Christian faith, but also by his philosophical understanding

that theology – and indeed all human knowledge – is historical in character. This meant that true learning could only proceed from the historical present, and on the foundation of the unavoidable personal standpoint of the one pursuing the study.

In other words, Ellacuría was working with the understanding that objectivity and authentic subjectivity are correlative and are unavoidably contextualised. Arising from that understanding, he was clear that, in the context of the violence and oppression of El Salvador, persecution would inevitably ensue. 'In a world where falsehood, injustice and oppression reign,' he wrote, 'a university that fights for truth, justice and freedom cannot fail to be persecuted.'

Ellacuría's expression of a contextualised Christian faith had its roots in a Church tradition that preceded Medellín, but which had gained momentum at the beginning of the 1960s, when the Church's teaching on social justice was developing rapidly. It is striking, for example, that while only two social encyclicals had appeared before 1960 – *Rerum novarum* in 1891 and *Quadragesimo anno* forty years later – three such encyclicals were published in quick succession in the 1960s: *Mater et magistra* (1961), *Pacem in terris* (1963) and *Populorum progressio* (1967). It is clear from these facts alone that the Catholic Church was adopting a more vigorous stance on behalf of social justice during that decade.

The Second Vatican Council (1962–65) also occurred during this period. One of its most inspiring documents was 'The Pastoral Constitution on the Church in the Modern World', written at the end of the council. The opening lines showed its ground-breaking tone and direction:

> The joy and hope, the grief and anguish of the people of our time, especially of those who are poor or afflicted in any way, are the joy and hope, the grief and anguish of the followers of Christ as well.

Its meaning was clear: Christian discipleship would not be authentic in the future unless it was open to the world as a historical reality, and structured by solidarity with the poor and afflicted.

The Latin American Church, especially, took this call of the council to heart. At Medellín it declared itself to be, not any kind of Church, but 'the Church in the present-day transformation of Latin America in the light of the Council'. At that time, ninety per cent of Latin Americans were Christian, and eighty per cent of them were economically poor. In that context, and in the light of the council's teaching, it was clear that Christian transformation had to involve a preferential option for the poor.

The manner in which the Latin American bishops interpreted the meaning of the council took on a worldwide significance when, in 1971, the bishops gathered in Rome for the third meeting of the Synod of Catholic Bishops of the World declared:

> Action on behalf of justice and participation in the transformation of the world fully appear to us as a constitutive dimension of the preaching of the Gospel, or, in other words, of the Church's mission for the redemption of the human race and its liberation from every oppressive structure.

The Response of the Jesuits

It was against this background of the Church's growing concern for and commitment to social justice and liberation from oppressive structures that the Thirty-Second General Congregation of the Jesuits was held from December 1974 to March 1975. Fully aware of its status as the highest authority in the Society of Jesus, the congregation firmly rooted the Jesuits' mission in the Church's commitment to faith-based social transformation. It did so by affirming the promotion of justice as 'an absolute requirement' of a Jesuit's service of faith. It also noted that this development was fully in harmony with the Jesuit charism, going back to St Ignatius himself.

Ellacuría must have felt strongly supported by the stance the congregation took. He had already played a leading role in moving the Central American Province towards Medellín's preferential option for the poor. At a major gathering of Jesuits on the Spiritual Exercises, held in 1969 for the Central American Province, he made a huge impact on those present by outlining how they were called to move forward after Medellín in the light of Ignatian spirituality. Several years later, this impact was reinforced when he gave a course on the Spiritual Exercises from a Latin American point of view. On that occasion, he was joined by another member of the UCA community, Jon Sobrino – the internationally renowned theologian, who only escaped assassination in 1989 because he was out of the country at the time.

Measured, therefore, by the Catholic Church's projection of its position in those years and by the mandate of the Thirty-Second General Congregation of the Society of Jesus, Ignacio Ellacuría and the members of his Jesuit community who died with him – Ignacio Martín-Baró, Segundo Montes, Amando López, Juan Ramón Moreno and Joaquin López y López – were clearly martyrs for the Catholic faith.

Influences on Ellacuría

Along with Ellacuría, the other leading figure at the historic event for Central American Jesuits in 1969 was Miguel Elizondo. He had been Ellacuría's director of novices, and was my Tertian director in Mexico in 1991–92. Elizondo, like Ellacuría, was a Basque. In 1947, as novice director, he went to El Salvador with a group of novices, among whom was Ignacio Ellacuría in his second year, to start a novitiate in that country. This meant that Ellacuría was influenced by the reality of El Salvador almost from the beginning of his Jesuit formation, and he identified with his adopted homeland so much that his life could be said to embody the words of scripture, 'Your people shall be my people' (Rt 1:16).

Ellacuría regarded Elizondo as one of the most important figures in his life. He would speak in a similar vein of the great German Jesuit theologian, Karl Rahner, with whom he studied in Austria, and of Xavier Zubiri, the Spanish philosopher who considered him his most gifted student and assistant. Other key figures for him were Pedro Arrupe, the superior general of the Jesuits who provided such inspiring global leadership in the aftermath of the council, and Oscar Romero, the martyred archbishop of El Salvador, now acknowledged as a saint.

A Mysticism of Open Eyes

Perhaps the greatest influence on Ellacuría was what can be called his 'mysticism of open eyes'. In that respect he was in the tradition of Bartolomé de las Casas (1484–1566), who has been called the Moses of liberation theology. Las Casas, a Dominican, was the great champion of the native people of Latin America who were being exploited by the European invaders. Appalled by the maltreatment of the native people, he used to say that in Latin America he had seen the scourged Christ of the Indies.

In similar language, Ellacuría used to speak of the need to take the crucified people of El Salvador down from their cross. This mysticism of open eyes – which was linked intimately with his Jesuit spirituality while also embedded in contemporary social reality – can be seen in a speech Ellacuría gave at the Jesuit-run University of Santa Clara, California, in 1982. He urged those present in Santa Clara to put to themselves the three questions St Ignatius asks in the First Week of his Spiritual Exercises, and to do so in front of a crucified world: what have I done for Christ? What am I doing now? And above all, what should I do? The answers, he said, 'lie both in your academic responsibility and in your personal responsibility'.

On another occasion, speaking in his native Spain about the situation in Latin America, he said, 'Turn your eyes and hearts toward these people who are suffering so much – some from misery and hunger and others from oppression and repression – and then [because I am a Jesuit] ... ask yourself, what have I done to crucify them? What can I do to take them down from the Cross? What can I do to resurrect them?' Contemplating the poor of El Salvador on their cross while engaged in contemplation of the crucified Christ, Ellacuría was led to see the Salvadoran reality with the eyes and the feelings evoked by Christ on Golgotha. This opened his capacity to love on to unexpected depths and unexpected dimensions of meaning and sensibility.

His loving was not glamorous or pleasurable. It could, instead, be painstaking and exhausting. It moved him to exercise his academic and personal responsibility by joining himself and the university with the economically poor and the victims of injustice, and to stay attached to them physically, mentally, intellectually, emotionally and spiritually. The bonds of that love were so deep and so courageous that nothing could break them: not the two periods of exile from El Salvador he endured, or the recurring threats of death; not the night the house was heavily gunned, or the two occasions when it was dynamited, or the bombing and destruction of valuable resources at the university, notably its printing press. He continued to give himself to those he loved with the result that in the end he died for, and with, them.

Identification with the Eucharistic Jesus

Ellacuría and his companions remind us of the Eucharistic Jesus celebrating the Passover meal with his family of disciples in the role of a Jewish father. By going down on his knees in love to wash his disciples' feet, Jesus emptied that role of its patriarchal dominance. Like Jesus, Ellacuría and companions came not to be served, but to serve (Mk 10:45). They were killed for living this liberated fatherhood of loving service, together with Julia Elba and he daughter Celina – women of the poor, who had come to the Jesuits for protection after their home had been damaged by a bomb just two days before.

Like their fellow Jesuit and good friend, Rutilio Grande, who had been martyred in El Salvador twelve years earlier on his way to celebrate Mass, Ellacuría and his companions remind us of Jesus, because no greater love is possible than to give one's life for others: 'This is my body, this is my blood, given for you'.

Two of the Jesuits were killed in their rooms. The others, including Ellacuría, were dragged from their beds, taken out to the garden, and killed while lying prostrate on the earth – evoking a time many years earlier when they lay prostrate on the ground during their priestly ordination ceremony. They were not afraid then to be vulnerable but, as they lay in the garden in the early hours of 16 November 1989, they knew that, for them, there would be no tomorrow on this earth; this was not only their Gethsemane, but also their Good Friday. They also believed, however, that while bullets could take their lives, their faith in the resurrection of Jesus gave them hope that beyond the tide of time their eternal alleluia had already begun. The high velocity bullets blasted their brains from their heads and scattered them on the grass. Some have conjectured that they were killed in this way to signify that the brains of the Jesuit university community were considered a danger to national security.

Connections with Ireland

Ignacio Ellacuría had connections with Ireland. He did his tertianship, the final year of his Jesuit formation, at Rathfarnham Castle at the start of the 1960s. Rathfarnham Castle at that time was a Jesuit residence and, as well as a tertianship, home to young Jesuits studying at University College, Dublin. Amando López, who would die with him, lived and did his theological studies at what was then the Jesuit House of Studies at Milltown Park, Dublin, where he was ordained in 1965. Later, in 1981, Ellacuría accompanied César Jerez, the charismatic leader of the Jesuits in Central America, to Dublin. They spoke to a gathering of Jesuits and friends in Milltown Park about the civil war then underway in El Salvador. (Jerez had stayed at Milltown Park on a previous visit to Dublin that I had helped to organise in 1980.) Jerez did most of the talking that evening, as he was more fluent in English than Ellacuría.

Years later, in 1991, a memorial bell was erected on the grounds of Milltown Park to honour the martyred Ignacio, his Jesuit community, Julia Elba and Celina, and also Archbishop Oscar Romero who had been martyred in 1980. It signified the solidarity of the Milltown Institute of Theology, Philosophy and Spirituality at Milltown Park with Ellacuria's vision of putting third-level education on the side of a faith that promotes justice and liberation from servitude.

Conclusion

Despite the horror and tragedy of that November dawn in 1989, the martyred Ellacuría and companions remain defiant; their deaths are a tribute to their lives. They remind us of their lives and make them even more inspiring. The deaths of these martyrs serve the lives of others by fostering vocations to the love they died for – the liberating love of a historically mediated salvation in diverse contexts. May Ignacio and companions rest in peace by inspiring us to go forth in faith to love the subordinated, the neglected, the exploited, the excluded and, in Ignacio's preferred term, the crucified of our countries. And may the risen Christ's love give us all, and our hopes and dreams, a future beyond the grave and urn. Amen! Alleluia!

ABOUT THE AUTHORS

Patrick Carberry SJ
Patrick Carberry SJ has served as rector of Clongowes Wood College, as novice master for the Irish Jesuits and as director of Manresa, the Irish Province's spirituality centre in Dollymount, Dublin. He was editor of *The Sacred Heart Messenger* on two occasions, and for nine years he was involved in the administration of the Irish Jesuit Province. At present, he is associate editor of Messenger Publications.

Brendan Carmody SJ
Brendan Carmody SJ is a Jesuit priest whose field of expertise is education. He spent many years in Zambia, where he taught in the university and worked as a government adviser. He has published widely on educational matters in Zambia, notably *Education in Zambia: Catholic Perspective* (1992) and *Conversion and Jesuit Schooling in Zambia* (1997). At present he lives in London where he is chaplain to the Tyburn Convent and visiting professor in St Mary University, Twickenham.

Errol Fernandes SJ
Errol Fernandes SJ is a member of the Bombay Province of the Society of Jesus. He was ordained in 1994, and pronounced his final vows in 2000. He is the author of six books, and has also released six CDs of his talks on a variety of themes. Besides teaching accountancy in St Xavier's College, Mumbai, he also teaches Scripture at various seminaries in India. He has travelled extensively, both in India and elsewhere, giving retreats, conferences and seminars.

Patrick Gallagher
Patrick Gallagher is a former Jesuit who, for some ten years, was a close friend and student of Fr John Hyde SJ, discussing philosophy, theology and spirituality. His understanding of Fr Hyde has been helped by the fact that he is an Irish speaker. He is now exploring

how his mentor's work can make a contribution to the modern world. The modern novel and, especially, Irish literature are among his wider interests. Married to a Canadian for forty-one years, they travel to Ireland each year.

John Looby SJ

Following his theological studies in Germany, John Looby SJ spent many years engaged in education in various capacities, most notably as senior English teacher in Clongowes Wood College, where he was renowned not only for his teaching but also for his creative theatrical productions. He was editor of *The Sacred Heart Messenger* from 2007 to 2013. In 2017, to mark the occasion of the beatification of Fr John Sullivan SJ, he wrote a biography of the new blessed, *A Man Sent by God*, which was published by Messenger Publications.

Thierry Meynard SJ

French Jesuit Thierry Meynard SJ is currently professor at Sun Yat-Sen University, Guangzhou, China, where he teaches Western Philosophy and Latin Classics, and also director of the Archive for the Introduction of Western Knowledge. From 2012–14, he was director of The Beijing Center for Chinese Studies, a study program established by the Jesuits in 1998. In 2003, he obtained his PhD in Philosophy from Peking University, after which he taught philosophy at Fordham University, New York. Since 2006, he has been a member of the Macau Ricci Institute. He has authored *The Jesuit Reading of Confucius* (2015), *The Religious Philosophy of Liang Shuming* (2011), *Confucius Sinarum Philosophus* (2011), and has co-authored with Sher-shiueh Li, Jesuit Chreia in Late Ming China (2014).

Thomas J. Morrissey SJ

Thomas J. Morrissey SJ is a Jesuit priest, educationalist, historian and author. Former headmaster of Crescent College Comprehensive, Limerick, and director of the National College of Industrial Relations, Dublin, he has taken his degrees from NUI. Among his twenty publications are *Towards a National University* (1983);

Peter Kenney SJ, 1779–1841: His Mission in Ireland and North America (1996); *William O'Brien, 1881–1968, Socialist, Dáil Deputy, Trade Union Leader* (2007) and *Laurence O'Neill, Lord Mayor of Dublin, 1917–1924* (2013). His latest work, *The Life and Times of Daniel Murray, Archbishop of Dublin, 1823–1852*, was published by Messenger Publications in 2017.

Fergus O'Donoghue SJ

Fergus O'Donoghue SJ studied history at University College Dublin before entering the Society of Jesus in 1970. After ordination, he went to Catholic University in Washington, DC, for studies in Church History. Fr O'Donoghue taught in Dublin at the Milltown Institute of Theology and Philosophy, where he was also Librarian. For ten years, he edited Studies, the Irish Jesuit quarterly review. He is now resident in Gonzaga College, Dublin, and ministers in the Church of the Miraculous Medal, Bird Avenue.

Gerry O'Hanlon SJ

Gerry O'Hanlon SJ is a Jesuit priest, theologian and former provincial of the Irish Jesuits. He taught for many years at the Milltown Institute, Dublin. He has lectured and written extensively on theological issues, especially Church reform and the role of the Church in the public square. His latest publications are *A Dialogue of Hope: Critical Thinking for Critical Times* (2017) and *The Quiet Revolution of Pope Francis: A Synodal Catholic Church in Ireland?* (2018), both published by Messenger Publications.

Kevin O'Higgins SJ

Kevin O'Higgins SJ is an Irish Jesuit who spent many years working in Paraguay, and who still retains a strong interest in all things to do with Latin American. His main activity over the past thirty years has been teaching philosophy. He is now director of the Jesuit University Support and Training (JUST) project in Ballymun, Dublin, which offers personal and academic support to people from the area who wish to pursue university-level studies.

Michael O'Sullivan SJ

Michael O'Sullivan SJ is recognised internationally as a leader in the academic study of applied spirituality. He is currently director of the Spirituality Institute for Research and Education in Dublin (SpIRE), and is programme leader of the MA in Applied Spirituality. He has lived and worked in Latin America, where he experienced first-hand the injustices endured by the poor. In 1991 he himself was prevented from entering El Salvador and, after detention under armed guard, deported to Nicaragua. Eventually he was able to return with the help of the Jesuits in El Salvador.

David Stewart SJ

A native of Scotland and member of the British Province, David Stewart SJ has worked at various times in secondary education, chaplaincy and young adult ministry. He has been superior of an international Jesuit community of scholastics in London, and is currently London correspondent for the US Jesuits' magazine, *America*. At present, he is director for England and Wales of the Pope's Worldwide Prayer Network, formerly known as the Apostleship of Prayer.

Gerard Whelan SJ

Following undergraduate studies in Trinity College, Dublin, Gerard Whelan SJ joined the Jesuits in 1982. After further philosophical studies, he went as a scholastic to Zambia and has lived abroad ever since. Upon completion of his initial theological studies in Hekima College, Nairobi, he studied for a doctorate in theology, after which he returned as lecturer to Nairobi, where he also assumed responsibility for a large Jesuit parish. Since 2007 he has been teaching theology in the Pontifical Gregorian University in Rome. In 2013 he published *Redeeming History: Social Concern in Bernard Lonergan and Robert Doran*.